STUDY GUIDE TO ACCOMPANY
Production/Operations Management
QUALITY, PERFORMANCE, AND VALUE
FIFTH EDITION

JAMES R. EVANS
UNIVERSITY OF CINCINNATI

PREPARED BY

CINDY HOUSE RANDALL
GEORGIA SOUTHERN UNIVERSITY

HUZEIFA MUSAJI
GEORGIA SOUTHERN UNIVERSITY

WEST PUBLISHING COMPANY

MINNEAPOLIS/ST. PAUL   NEW YORK   LOS ANGELES   SAN FRANCISCO

WEST'S COMMITMENT TO THE ENVIRONMENT

In 1906, West Publishing Company began recycling materials left over from the production of books. This began a tradition of efficient and responsible use of resources. Today, 100% of our legal bound volumes are printed on acid-free, recycled paper consisting of 50% new fibers. West recycles nearly 27,700,000 pounds of scrap paper annually—the equivalent of 229,300 trees. Since the 1960s, West has devised ways to capture and recycle waste inks, solvents, oils, and vapors created in the printing process. We also recycle plastics of all kinds, wood, glass, corrugated cardboard, and batteries, and have eliminated the use of polystyrene book packaging. We at West are proud of the longevity and the scope of our commitment to the environment.

West pocket parts and advance sheets are printed on recyclable paper and can be collected and recycled with newspapers. Staples do not have to be removed. Bound volumes can be recycled after removing the cover.

Production, Prepress, Printing and Binding by West Publishing Company.

COPYRIGHT © 1997 by WEST PUBLISHING CO.
                                610 Opperman Drive
                                P.O. Box 64526
                                St. Paul, MN 55164–0526

All rights reserved
Printed in the United States of America
04 03 02 01 00 99 98 97   8 7 6 5 4 3 2 1 0

ISBN 0–314–06248–3

Contents

Part I: Foundations
Chapter 1: Introduction to Production and Operations Management 1
Chapter 2: Managing for Quality and High Performance 9
Chapter 3: P/OM and Strategic Planning 17
Chapter 4: Measuring Operations Performance 25
Chapter 5: Work Design and Human Resource Management 33

Part II: Strategic Issues in Operations
Chapter 6: Product Design and Development 41
Chapter 7: Forecasting and Capacity Planning 53
Chapter 8: Facility Location and Distribution System Design 71

Part III: Designing and Managing Production Processes
Chapter 9: Process Technology and Design 81
Chapter 10: Facility Layout and Workplace Design 95
Chapter 11: Process Management 107
Chapter 12: Statistical Quality Control 119

Part IV: Managing Materials
Chapter 13: Materials and Inventory Management 127
Chapter 14: Decision Models for Inventory Management 141
Chapter 15: Lean Production and Synchronous Manufacturing 149

Part V: Planning and Scheduling
Chapter 16: Aggregate Production Planning and Master Scheduling 157
Chapter 17: Material Requirements Planning 169
Chapter 18: Operations Scheduling and Production-Activity Control 181
Chapter 19: Project Planning, Scheduling, and Control 193

Supplementary Chapters
Supplement A: Computer Simulation 203
Supplement B: Decision Analysis 217
Supplement C: Waiting-Line Models 227
Supplement D: Linear Programming 237
Supplement E: Transportation Problem 245

Chapter 1
Introduction to Production and Operations Management

LEARNING OBJECTIVES

Chapter 1 is an introduction to Production and Operations Management. It explains the concept, scope and purpose of P/OM in service organizations as well as in manufacturing. The importance of P/OM in creating customer value, the activities for which operations managers are responsible, the structure of production systems, and the evolution of P/OM are key topics that are discussed in the chapter. The student should concentrate attention in the following areas:

- What activities do the terms production and operation encompass?

- Why is P/OM necessary?

- What can companies do to compete in the global marketplace?

- How do traditional and new management paradigm differ?

- What are the activities of operations management?

- How can P/OM activities be classified?

- What is a production system and what are its components?

- How is a production system affected by its environment?

2 PART I: FOUNDATIONS

- How has P/OM evolved in the last century?
- What is the Quality Revolution?
- What is the focus of lean production?
- What does soft manufacturing enable companies to do?
- What are the challenges facing modern P/OM?
- How does a global economy affect management?
- How can firms be leaders in a global marketplace?

GLOSSARY

PRODUCTION	The conversion of resources into goods and services.
OPERATIONS	The activities associated with the production of goods and services.
PRODUCTION/OPERATIONS MANAGEMENT (P/OM)	Managing the resources needed to produce goods and services.
OPERATIONS MANAGEMENT	Another term for P/OM.
PRODUCTION SYSTEM	The collection of all interrelated activities and operations in producing goods and services.
SERVICE	A social act which takes place in direct contact between customer and representatives of the service company.
CONSUMERS	Those persons who ultimately purchase a firm's final goods and services.
EXTERNAL CUSTOMER	Any department or firm which adds value to a product before the product reaches the consumer.
INTERNAL CUSTOMER	The recipients of goods and services from internal suppliers.
PROCESS	A sequence of activities that is intended to produce a certain result for a customer.

CHAPTER 1: INTRODUCTION TO PRODUCTION AND OPERATIONS MANAGEMENT

LEAN PRODUCTION — New approaches for managing manufacturing systems that streamline interdependent functions.

TOTAL CYCLE TIME — A time that begins when the customer expresses a need and ends when the customer happily pays a company.

VALUE — Quality coupled with price.

GLOBAL INTEGRATION — The coordination and balancing of global resources.

WORLD-CLASS — A status achieved in the global marketplace by meeting consumer demands in price, quality, and time at low costs.

SELF-TEST QUESTIONS

MULTIPLE CHOICE

1. The term operations refers to the activities of:

   A. Planning, leading, directing and controlling.
   B. Marketing, financing, purchasing and accounting.
   C. Manufacturing, transportation, supply or service.
   D. Machining, drilling, polishing and packaging.

2. The major components of a production system include:

   A. Inputs and outputs.
   B. Suppliers and customers.
   C. Processes.
   D. Managers and feedback.
   E. All of the above.

3. In the late 1980's, a major study concluded that the United States had lost its ability to compete because:

   A. Marketing and finance were underemphasized.
   B. Organizations were trying to integrate design, manufacturing, and marketing.
   C. Underinvestment in research and development, facilities, and employee development.
   D. Consumer needs were changing too quickly.
   E. All of the above.

4 PART I: FOUNDATIONS

4. Which of the following is **NOT** a major concern of today's Operations Manager?

   A. Quality.
   B. Time - Based Competition.
   C. Globalization.
   D. All of the above are important. ✓

5. One way of putting the operations management function into a useful framework is to classify P/OM activities into the following hierarchy:

   A. Top management, middle management, and workers/supervisors.
   B. Strategic, tactical, and operational. ✓
   C. Service and manufacturing.
   D. Receiving, conversion, subassembly, final assembly, packaging and shipping.

6. Leaders in the global marketplace will be world-class firms that:

   A. Train and empower employees to make continuous improvements.
   B. Make use of total quality management approaches.
   C. Set standards that other companies try to meet or beat.
   D. Seek to minimize cycle times.
   E. All of the above. ✓

7. The sequence of activities, or processes, that is intended to produce a certain result for a customer is:

   A. Receiving, subassembly, conversion, final assembly, packaging and shipping.
   B. Conversion, receiving, subassembly, packaging, final assembly, and shipping.
   C. Receiving, conversion, subassembly, final assembly, packaging and shipping. ✓
   D. Subassembly, conversion, receiving, final assembly, packaging, and shipping.

8. Contemporary operations management activities include:

   A. Understanding customer needs.
   B. Exploiting technology to respond to customer requirements.
   C. Motivating and educating employees.
   D. All of the above. ✓
   E. A and C but not B.

9. To achieve world-class status:

   A. Quality must be improved regardless of manufacturing costs.
   B. The roles of finance and manufacturing must be integrated.
   C. Suppliers must be motivated. ✓
   D. The operations manager must play a critical role. ✓

CHAPTER 1: INTRODUCTION TO PRODUCTION AND OPERATIONS MANAGEMENT 5

10. Value:

   A. Is defined by quality and price.
   B. Has forced many companies to rethink service.
   C. Motivates consumers to buy regardless of price.
   D. All of the above.
   (E.) A and B but not C.

TRUE/FALSE

1. T Babbage believed that the total cost of a product could be lowered by hiring workers with different skills and paying them according to their expertise.

2. F Strategic planning involves a short-time horizon, such as one year, and a low degree of uncertainty and risk.

3. F An "internal" customer is an employee who is a major purchaser of the firm's products.

4. T Frederick Taylor believed that management should be concerned with the planning, directing and organizing work while workers should carry out their assigned tasks.

5. T W. Edwards Deming is credited with teaching the Japanese about the need and benefits of improved product quality.

6. F As the goals of low cost and high product quality become "givens," companies began placing emphasis on marketing and finance to gain a competitive advantage.

7. F Some companies may choose to operate centrally within regional boundaries and will still have access to essential markets.

8. F P/OM principles are not only very complicated, they require discipline and vision to implement.

9. T The purpose of operations management is to deliver ever-improving value for customers through the continuous improvement of overall company performance and capabilities.

10. T Soft manufacturing blends automation and computing technology, allowing companies to customize and produce single quantities of products at mass-production speeds.

6 PART I: FOUNDATIONS

FILL IN THE BLANK

1. _Global Integration_ is the coordination and balancing of global resources.

2. The streamlining of interdependent functions is known as _Lean Manufacturing_.

3. The _Quality Revolution_ began in the United States in 1980 when NBC televised a program featuring Deming and his role in transforming Japanese industry.

4. _Soft Manuf_ blends automation and computing technology, allowing companies to customize and produce single quantities of products at mass-production speed.

5. The time needed to meet a customer's requirement is the _total time Cycle_.

6. _Service_ is a social act which takes place in direct contact between the customer and representatives of the service company.

7. A _Process_ is a sequence of activities that is intended to produce a certain result for a customer.

8. The recipients of goods and services from internal suppliers are called _Internal Customers_.

9. The new management paradigm views a business enterprise as a _total system_, in which activities are to be coordinated not only vertically throughout an organization, but also horizontally across multiple functions.

10. Quality coupled with price defines the notion of _Value_.

Chapter 1: Introduction to Production and Operations Management

Key to Self-Test Questions

Multiple Choice

1. C
2. E
3. C
4. D
5. B
6. E
7. C
8. D
9. D
10. E

True/False

1. T
2. F
3. F
4. T
5. T
6. F
7. F
8. F
9. T
10. T

Fill in the Blank

1. Global integration
2. lean production
3. quality revolution
4. soft manufacturing
5. total time cycle
6. Service
7. process
8. internal customers
9. total system
10. value

Chapter 2
Managing for Quality and High Performance

LEARNING OBJECTIVES

*C*hapter 2 presents principles that will improve customer value. In presenting these principles, the importance, scope and fundamental elements of TQM (total quality management) is discussed. Comparisons are made between the philosophies of Deming, Juran and Crosby. You are shown how the Malcolm Baldrige Quality Award is used as a model and tool for TQM. This award's criteria is contrasted with the ISO 9000 quality system standards. This chapter shows how these factors, and others, contribute to the implementation of TQM within an organization. Concentrate on the following:

- What is productivity? What cycle is spawned by low productivity?

- How does quality affect cost?

- What are the key principles of TQM?

- What are the benefits of TQM?

- What is the scope of quality management?

- What is quality? How can it be imposed on an organization?

- How does the nature of quality differ in service and manufacturing?

- ✦ What were the philosophies of Deming, Juran and Crosby?
- ✦ What are the elements of TQM?
- ✦ What are the purposes of the Malcolm Baldrige National Quality Award? Upon what criteria is it based? What has been the impact of the award?
- ✦ What are the ISO 9000 series of standards?
- ✦ What is the QS 9000 and what does it represent?
- ✦ How can TQM be implemented?

Glossary

PRODUCTIVITY	A measure of the extent to which the resources of an organization are being used effectively in transforming inputs to outputs. A ratio: output divided by input.
HIDDEN FACTORY	That portion of the plant capacity used to rework parts and products recalled from customers and to retest and reinspect rejected units. This part of the plant exists solely because of poor quality.
TOTAL QUALITY MANAGEMENT (TQM)	An integrative management concept directed as continuous improvement in the quality of goods and services by involving all levels and functions of the organization.
SPECIFICATIONS	Design characteristics that are defined by targets and tolerances.
QUALITY COUNCIL	A steering committee of senior managers. These councils assume many responsibilities, including incorporating TQM into strategic planning process and coordinating the overall effort.
QUALITY TRILOGY	The three major quality processes on which Juran focuses. These are quality planning, quality control and quality improvement.

CHAPTER 2: MANAGING FOR QUALITY AND HIGH PERFORMANCE

SELF-TEST QUESTIONS

MULTIPLE CHOICE

1. Which of the following is **NOT** the result of a low rate of productivity growth?

    A. Fewer units produced per input.
    B. Higher prices for goods and services.
    C. Higher revenues.
    D. Unused capacity and lower unemployment.
    E. All of the above result from a low rate of productivity growth.

2. The ISO 9000 standards:

    A. Cover similar registration requirements as the Baldrige award.
    B. Were intended to be advisory in nature and to be used in two-party contractual situations and for internal audits.
    C. Specify a measure of quality performance.
    D. Requires little documentation.
    E. Were drawn up by The Big Three automobile manufacturers.

3. The Hidden Factory:

    A. Can account for up to 10% of a plant's total capacity.
    B. Exists because of poor customer relations.
    C. Is the portion of plant capacity that exists to rework unsatisfactory parts.
    D. Is necessary because building quality into a product costs a company so much more.
    E. Has been created because products have more complicated features and need more repairs.

4. The term total quality management:

    A. Conveys a company wide effort to achieve customer satisfaction.
    B. Involves the entire work force.
    C. Involves customers as well as suppliers.
    D. Focuses on continuous improvement.
    E. All of the above are correct.

5. Crosby's Basic Elements of Improvement are:

   A. Quality planning, quality control, and quality improvement.
   B. Determination, education, and implementation.
   C. Leadership, cooperation, learning, process management, improvement, employee fulfillment, and customer satisfaction.
   D. Product and service conformance to specification by reducing uncertainty and variability in the design and manufacturing process.

6. When comparing the ISO 9000 and the Baldrige Award criteria:

   A. The Baldrige Award and the ISO 9000 registration cover similar requirements.
   B. Both address improvements and results.
   C. Both are forms of achievement recognition.
   D. Are distinctly different instruments that can reinforce each other when properly used.
   E. All of the above are true.

7. Continuous improvement:

   A. Is sought only in providing better products and services.
   B. Does not mean that a company is more responsive and efficient.
   C. Means improvement as part of daily operations and of all work units of a company.
   D. Cannot be measured by improvement in cycle-time performance.
   E. All of the above.

8. Which of the following is **NOT** a purpose of the Malcolm Baldrige National Quality Award?

   A. To help stimulate U.S. companies to improve quality and productivity.
   B. To recognize achievements of those companies that improve quality of their goods and services.
   C. To establish guidelines and criteria that can be used evaluate quality improvement efforts.
   D. To provide specific guidance for other U.S. enterprises that wish to learn how to manage for high quality.
   E. All of the above are purposes of the award.

9. TQM benefits all organizations by:

   A. Reducing waste and inventory.
   B. Improving customer satisfaction through better and more reliable goods and services.
   C. Increasing flexibility in meeting market demands.
   D. Reducing work in process and improving delivery times.
   E. All of the above are correct.

10. Which of the following statements is **NOT** a key principle of TQM?
    A. Satisfy the needs of the customers.
    B. Correct problems as soon as they can be detected.
    C. Develop an attitude of continuous improvement in everyone.
    D. Understand the value of measuring performance to identify opportunities and maintain improvements.
    E. Eliminate sources of inefficiencies and costs.

TRUE/FALSE

1. Higher quality always leads to higher costs and higher prices.

2. The U.S. no longer ranks first in productivity among nations.

3. Productivity is the ratio of the output of a production process to the inputs used.

4. Profitability is sensitive to changes in both productivity and quality.

5. <u>Targets</u> are ideal values for which production is expected to strive.

6. <u>Conform</u> <u>to</u> <u>specifications</u> measures how well a product conforms to consumer expectations.

7. The term <u>fitness for use</u> relates to how a quality product or service meets (or exceeds) customer requirements and expectations.

8. Deming identifies two sources of improvement in any process: elimination of "common causes" of variation inherent in the system as well as "special causes" of variation caused by specific machines, men or materials.

9. Customer needs and performance standards are often difficult to identify and measure, primarily because the customer defines them, and each customer is different.

10. Juran advocates the accounting and analysis of quality costs to direct attention to quality problems.

14 PART I: FOUNDATIONS

FILL IN THE BLANK

1. The standards for ISO 9000 are based on the principle that quality should be defined by the product or service's _____ _____ _____, and that the customer is the one who decides on that definition.

2. _____ are design characteristics that are defined by targets and tolerances.

3. _____ _____ is a steering committee of senior managers which assumes many responsibilities, including incorporating TQM into strategic planning process and coordinating the overall effort.

4. Juran's _____ _____ focuses on three major quality processes: quality planning, quality control, and quality improvement.

5. Crosby's program differs from Juran and Deming's in that his program is primarily _____.

6. Fact-based management is built upon a framework of _____, _____, and _____.

7. _____ management commitment and leadership is the key driver in the successful implementation of TQM.

8. The scoring system for the Baldrige Award is based upon three evaluation dimensions: _____, _____, and _____.

9. _____ are ideal values for which production is expected to strive.

10. Deming focused on the improvement of product and service conformance to specifications by reducing _____ and _____ in the design and manufacturing process.

Chapter 2: Managing for Quality and High Performance

Key to Self-Test Questions

Multiple Choice

1. C
2. B
3. C
4. E
5. B
6. D
7. C
8. E
9. E
10. B

True/False

1. F
2. F
3. T
4. T
5. T
6. F
7. T
8. F
9. T
10. T

Fill in the Blank

1. fitness for purpose
2. Specifications
3. Quality Council
4. Quality Trilogy
5. behavioral
6. measurement; information; analysis
7. Top
8. approach; deployment; results
9. Targets
10. uncertainty; variability

Chapter 3
P/OM and Strategic Planning

LEARNING OBJECTIVES

*C*hapter 3 focuses on strategic planning, which in turn affects corporate strategy. Corporate strategy is composed of marketing and sales strategy, design strategy, and operations strategy. These strategies help the organization develop capabilities for achieving a competitive advantage. In the past, operations strategy has been neglected as companies focus on financial and marketing perspectives. This chapter discusses strategic planning and operations strategy. Concentrate on the following:

- What is the scope of Strategic Planning?

- What is a corporate strategy and its components?

- What is competitive advantage and how can it be achieved?

- What are the two basic types of competitive strategy?

- How can a company build a competitive advantage?

- How can quality be integrated into strategic business planning?

- What are the components of operations strategy?

- How can an operations strategy be applied to service organizations? To manufacturing organizations?

◆ What are the common approaches for strategy formation and implementation?

Glossary

CORPORATE STRATEGY	A strategy which defines the businesses in which the corporation will participate and also develops plans for the acquisition and allocation of resources among these businesses. Environmental factors such as customer demand, labor supply, material sources, capital sources, and a company's or competitor's strengths and weaknesses are considered.
STRATEGIC PLANNING	The determination of the long-term goals, policies, and plans for an organization. It involves defining the basic philosophy of the organization, identifying its competitive advantage and growth direction, determining the products and services to be provided, and planning for the acquisition and allocation of critical resources.
STRATEGIC BUSINESS UNITS (SBUs)	Families of products having similar characteristics or methods of production.
COMPETITIVE ADVANTAGE	A firm's ability to achieve superiority over its competitors by offering better customer value.
DISTINCTIVE COMPETENCIES	Strengths that are unique to a company. These could be a highly skilled work force, a strong distribution system, or the ability to rapidly develop new products or change production-output rates.
FLEXIBILITY	The capacity of a production system to adapt successfully to changing environmental conditions and process requirements.
VARIETY	Refers to a company's ability to produce a wide range of products and options.
PRODUCT LEAD TIME	The total time required by a company to deliver a finished product that satisfies customers' needs.
OPERATIONS STRATEGY	This strategy sets parameters for how the firm's resources will be converted into goods and services that meet design specifications.

MANUFACTURING STRATEGY	The way the capabilities of the manufacturing function are developed to support the desired competitive advantage of the business units and to complement the efforts of other functions.
STRATEGIC SERVICE VISION	A service strategy that integrates both marketing and operations. It should focus on identifying a target market segment, develop a service concept that addresses customers' needs, designing an operating strategy to support service, and designing a delivery system to support operating strategy.
CUSTOMER CONTACT	The physical presence of the customer in the system.
MISSION	Defines a firm's reason for existence.
VISION	Describes where the organization is headed, where it intends to be in the future.
GUIDING PRINCIPLES	The attitudes and policies that need to be followed by all employees at all levels of the organization in order for the vision to be realized.

SELF-TEST QUESTIONS

MULTIPLE CHOICE

1. The three basic components of corporate strategy are:

    A. Accounting, marketing, and manufacturing.
    B. Finance, marketing, and operations.
    C. Marketing and sales, design, and operations.
    D. Finance, sales, and operations.

2. When operations is **NOT** considered a factor of the corporate strategy:

    A. Productivity and quality have suffered.
    B. Plans are developed from primarily financial and marketing perspectives.
    C. Operations managers can only react to strategic plans.
    D. The organization's long-term success is threatened.
    E. All of the above.

3. Which of the following statements is **NOT** true of a company trying to gain a competitive advantage as a low-cost industry leader:

   A. Produce high volumes of mature products.
   B. Have low costs that result from low productivity.
   C. Have high capacity utilization.
   D. Has long production runs of a narrow model range with little customization.
   E. Infrequent design changes.

4. To use the differentiation strategy successfully:

   A. A firm must be unique in its industry along some dimension that is widely valued by customers.
   B. A firm does not have to have a flexible operations strategy.
   C. The firm does not have to concentrate on cost.
   D. None of the above.

5. Which of the following is **NOT** a quality-related dimension on which a company might would choose to concentrate:

   A. Product design.
   B. Service.
   C. High flexibility and variety.
   D. Innovation.
   E. None of the above.

6. A strategic service vision focuses on the following elements:

   A. Target market identification.
   B. Developing a service concept to address customers' needs.
   C. Designing an operating strategy to support service.
   D. Designing a delivery system to support the operating strategy.
   E. All of the above.

7. When comparing high-contact and low-contact systems and how they impact performance criteria for operations, it can be said that:

   A. Efficiency is of more concern to high-contact systems.
   B. Cost reduction through economies of scale is easier in a high-contact system.
   C. Low-contact systems are more amenable to statistical methods of process-quality control.
   D. The presence of the customer makes quality control more difficult for low-contact systems.
   E. Flexibility is more important in low-contact systems.

8. Which of the following is **NOT** an advantage of short product lead time:

   A. Penetrate new markets rapidly.
   B. Cost savings in development time.
   C. Introduce new products more rapidly.
   D. Increases importance of long-term sales forecasts.
   E. Reduction of inventory.

9. **NOT** included in a company's product lead time is the time spent on:

   A. Design and engineering.
   B. Purchasing and manufacturing.
   C. Marketing and selling.
   D. Testing, packaging and shipping.
   E. None of the above.

10. Operations strategy consists of the following components:

    A. Product technology.
    B. Capacity and facilities and location.
    C. Human resources.
    D. Process technology, operating decisions and integration of suppliers.
    E. Quality.
    F. All of the above.

TRUE/FALSE

1. Strategic planning involves issues that have a short-run impact on the firm.

2. The design strategy determines how the firm will match its technological capabilities with market needs to develop specifications for competitively priced goods and services.

3. Cost leadership is most effective when you are marketing an inferior product.

4. We use the term competitive advantage to refer to a firm's ability to compete consistently on lower costs and a resultant low price.

5. Time has come to be recognized as one of the most important sources of competitive advantage in recent years.

6. In most companies, complete integration of TQM into strategic business planning occurs only when decreasing profits demand it.

22   PART I: FOUNDATIONS

7. The subject of a manufacturing strategy is the product that is manufactured or the service that is provided.

8. Guiding principles define attitudes and policies that need to be followed by upper management in order for the vision to be realized.

9. Business strategy has traditionally been dominated by either finance or marketing considerations.

10. Flexibility is the capacity of a production system to adapt successfully to changing environmental conditions and process requirements.

FILL IN THE BLANK

1. The three core elements of <u>business strategy</u> are the _____, _____, and _____.

2. The _____ strategy sets parameters for how the firm's resources will be converted into goods and services that meet the design specifications.

3. We use the term _____ _____ to denote a firm's ability to achieve market superiority over its competitors.

4. There are two basic types of competitive strategy: _____ and _____.

5. As the average level of product quality has increased overall among competitors, consumers are turning toward _____ as the primary means of differentiating among firms.

6. Firms on the leading edge of product technology usually focus and _____ and _____ as a core component of their strategy.

7. _____ is the measure of the amount of output that can be produced over a period of time.

8. The question "Why are we in business?" is answered in the company's _____ statement.

9. _____ _____ is the pointing, or aligning, of the entire organization in a common direction.

10. _____ is a negotiation process in which leaders communicate midterm objectives and measure to middle managers, who develop short-term objectives and recommend necessary resources, targets, and roles or responsibilities. These are then discussed and debated until an agreement is reached.

KEY TO SELF-TEST QUESTIONS

MULTIPLE CHOICE

1. C
2. E
3. B
4. A
5. D
6. E
7. C
8. D
9. C
10. F

TRUE/FALSE

1. F
2. T
3. F
4. F
5. T
6. T
7. F
8. F
9. T
10. T

FILL IN THE BLANK

1. finance; marketing; and operations
2. operations
3. competitive advantage
4. low-cost; differentiation
5. service
6. research; development
7. Capacity
8. mission
9. Policy deployment
10. Catchball

Chapter 4
Measuring Operations Performance

LEARNING OBJECTIVES

Chapter 4 describes how operations managers measure the performance of their operations. These measurements enable managers to make decisions on facts, not opinions. You are shown how the scope of performance measurement has evolved from the traditional financial considerations to customer related quality measures. Different types of measurements are presented and procedure for developing good performance indicators is introduced. Finally, important issues related to measuring customer satisfaction, productivity, and quality costs are discussed. Concentrate on the following:

- What is the scope of performance measurement?

- How is service quality different from manufacturing quality?

- What are the five key dimensions used to assess service quality?

- What are the two categories of measurements?

- What are the elements of a good performance indicator?

- What are the steps involved in developing useful performance measures?

- Why is it important to measure customer satisfaction?

26   PART I: FOUNDATIONS

✦ What are the different ways by which one can measure productivity?

✦ What is a productivity index?

✦ What are the various classifications of quality costs?

GLOSSARY

SUPPLIERS (VENDORS)	Providers of goods and services that may be used in the production, delivery, and use of a company's own products and services.
DEFECT	A term used interchangeably with "nonconformity" and is the number of nonconformities per unit. It is a common indicator of manufacturing quality.
TANGIBLES	A way by which consumers assess service quality. Examples are physical facilities, equipment, and appearance of employees.
RELIABILITY	A way by which consumers assess service quality. The ability of an organization to perform the promised service dependably and accurately.
RESPONSIVENESS	A way by which consumers assess service quality. The willingness to help customers and provide prompt service.
ASSURANCE	A way by which consumers assess service quality. The knowledge and courtesy of employees, and their ability to inspire trust and confidence in customers.
EMPATHY	A way by which consumers assess service quality. The amount of caring and individualized attention the firm provides to its customers.
ATTRIBUTE MEASUREMENT	The measurement of a characteristic that assumes one of two values.
VARIABLE MEASUREMENT	The measurement of those characteristics that can be measured on a continuous scale.

Chapter 4: Measuring Operations Performance

Key Business Factors	Factors that are important to the success of the business and affect strategic planning, design and management of process quality, human resources development and management, and data collection and analysis.
Total Productivity	A measure of the ratio of total output to total input. This measure does not show the interaction between each input and output separately and thus is too broad to be used as a tool for improving specific areas of operations.
Multifactor Productivity	The ratio of total output to a subset of inputs. This measure may ignore important inputs and thus may not accurately reflect overall productivity.
Partial-Factor Productivity	A measure of the ratio of total output to a single input. This measure provides useful information about specific processes.
Productivity Index	The ratio of productivity measured in some time period to the productivity in a base period. By tracking such indexes over time, managers can evaluate the success (or lack of success) of various projects and decisions.
Cost of Quality	Costs associated with avoiding poor quality or those incurred as a result of poor quality.
Prevention Costs	Costs associated with preventing nonconforming products from being made and reaching the customer.
Appraisal Costs	Costs associated with assessing the level of quality attained by an operating system and detecting and correcting problems.
Internal-Failure Costs	Costs incurred as a result of unsatisfactory quality that is found before the delivery of a product to the customer.
External-Failure Costs	Costs incurred due to poor quality products reaching the customers.
Pareto Analysis	A useful analysis tool for quality-cost data. It identifies the "vital few" causes of quality problems, which when corrected, will have a high return for a low dollar input.
Measurement Reliability	The extent to which a measuring instrument consistently measures the "true value" of the characteristic being measured.
Interlinking	The quantitative modeling of cause-and-effect relationships between external and internal performance criteria.

SELF-TEST QUESTIONS

MULTIPLE CHOICE

1. Which of the following is **NOT** a performance measurement that managers should focus on in a production system model?

    A. Supplier performance.
    B. Customer satisfaction.
    C. Product and service quality.
    D. Business and support services.
    E. Company operational performance.

2. Which of the following is **NOT** a benefit of using certified suppliers?

    A. Makes inspections unnecessary.
    B. Reduces the number of suppliers used.
    C. Gives the suppliers an incentive for continuously improving quality and service to their customer organizations to attract more business.
    D. Reduces inventory.
    E. All of the above are true.

3. Companies usually classify defects as:

    A. Critical.
    B. Unusual.
    C. Detrimental.
    D. Allowable.
    E. Controllable.

4. Which of the following is **NOT** a general dimension of service quality?

    A. Tangibles.
    B. Reliability.
    C. Responsiveness.
    D. Durability.
    E. Empathy.

5. Data that can be measured on a continuous scale is referred to as:

    A. Attribute data.
    B. Quantifiable data.
    C. Variable data.
    D. Measurable data.
    E. Reliable data.

6. Which of the following statements is **FALSE** about attribute data measurement?

    A. They indicate the degree of conformance to specifications.
    B. Inspection by attributes is usually simpler than inspection by variables.
    C. Attribute inspection is less efficient than variable inspection.
    D. Attribute inspection requires a larger sample to obtain the same amount of statistical information.
    E. Is a characteristic of quality that is either present or absent in the product under consideration.

7. Good performance indicators should:

    A. Be strongly related to customer satisfaction.
    B. Be easy to understand and interpret.
    C. Provide factual assistance for decision making.
    D. Be a basis for comparative analysis and be economical to apply.
    E. All of the above.

8. Which of the following is **NOT** a step in the process for generating useful performance measures?

    A. Identify all customers of the system and determine their requirements and expectations.
    B. Define the work process that provides the product or service.
    C. Define the value-adding activities and outputs that comprise the process.
    D. Evaluate the usefulness of each performance measure.
    E. Identify all suppliers of the system and determine their requirements and expectations.

9. Product liability costs is an example of:

    A. Internal failure costs.
    B. External failure costs.
    C. Prevention costs.
    D. Appraisal costs.
    E. None of the above.

10. Knowledgeable and courteous front-line personnel is an example of which of the following service quality dimensions?

    A. Reliability.
    B. Tangibles.
    C. Responsiveness.
    D. Assurance.
    E. Empathy.

TRUE/FALSE

1. The number of nonconformities per unit is a common indicator of manufacturing quality.

2. Errors per opportunity is the measure of quality used by service organizations.

3. A minor defect is one that is not critical but is likely to materially reduce the usability of the unit for its intended purpose.

4. Inspection by variables is usually simpler than inspection by attributes because it can be done more quickly and easily as less information needs to be recorded.

5. Partial factor productivity uses the ratio of total output to a subset of input.

6. Total productivity ratios do not show the interaction between each input and output separately and thus are too broad to be used as a tool for improving specific areas of operations.

7. Productivity is a relative measure and it must be compared to something to be meaningful.

8. Cost of quality are costs associated with avoiding poor quality or those incurred as a result of poor quality.

9. Downgrading costs are external failure costs that result from revenues lost by selling a product at a lower price because it does not meet specifications.

10. Customer satisfaction measurement should include both the <u>importance</u> and the <u>performance</u> of key quality characteristics.

Chapter 4: Measuring Operations Performance   31

FILL IN THE BLANK

1. _____ is a term used to describe providers of goods and services that may be used at any stage in the production, delivery, and use of a company's own products and services.

2. _____ is the ability of a service organization to perform the promised service dependably and accurately.

3. _____ is a characteristic of quality that is either present or absent in the unit or product under consideration.

4. The elements of business that affect strategic planning, design and management of process quality, human resources development and management, and data collection and analysis are referred to as _____ _____ _____.

5. A _____ _____ is the ratio of productivity measured in some time period to the productivity in a base period.

6. _____ costs are those expended to keep non-conforming products from being made and reaching the customer.

7. _____ _____ is how well the measuring instrument consistently measures the "true value" of the characteristic being measured.

8. The quantitative modeling of cause-and-effect relationship between external and internal performance criteria is called _____.

9. _____ is the ratio of the time needed to perform a task to some predetermined "standard time".

10. _____ _____ is a useful analysis tool for quality-cost data and it indicates the "vital few" improvements that will have the greatest effect on the overall quality.

KEY TO SELF-TEST QUESTIONS

MULTIPLE CHOICE

1. B   5. C   9. B
2. D   6. A   10. D
3. A   7. E
4. D   8. E

TRUE/FALSE

1. T   5. F   9. F
2. T   6. T   10. T
3. F   7. T
4. F   8. T

FILL IN THE BLANK

1. Suppliers or Vendors
2. Reliability
3. Attribute
4. key business factors
5. productivity index
6. Prevention
7. Measurement reliability
8. interlinking
9. Efficiency
10. Pareto analysis

Chapter 5
Work Design and Human Resource Management

LEARNING OBJECTIVES

*C**hapter 5* focuses on the managing and designing of high-performance systems. This chapter examines changes in the nature of work and how these changes affect the management of operations, the roles that leadership and empowerment play in operations management, and the design and use of high-performance work systems. You should concentrate on the following:

- ✦ What are the principal resources of all businesses?

- ✦ How has the nature of worked changed? How have management philosophies changed?

- ✦ What can operations managers do to foster high-performance work systems?

- ✦ How do leadership and empowerment help create high-performance systems?

- ✦ How are high-performance systems designed? What is an effective job design?

- ✦ Why is motivation an important consideration in work design?

- ✦ How do high-performance work environments provide opportunities for job enlargement and job enrichment?

34 PART I: FOUNDATIONS

- ✦ Why are teams critical in designing high-performance systems? How are teams beneficial? What are the more common types of teams?

- ✦ What are quality circles and for what are they used? Why have many efforts to use quality circles failed in the United States?

- ✦ What is a self-managed team and what are its features?

- ✦ Why are rewards and recognitions important and what types should be used?

- ✦ Why are training and education critical for high-performance systems?

Glossary

HIGH-PERFORMANCE WORK SYSTEMS	Denotes job and organization designs that lead not only to high levels of performance, but also to greater flexibility and more rapid response to changing customer requirements.
LEADERSHIP	The right to exercise authority and the ability to achieve results from people and systems under one's authority.
EMPOWERMENT	The giving of authority to employees to make decisions, gain greater control over their work, and thus more easily satisfy customers.
JOB	The set of tasks an individual performs.
JOB DESIGN	Involves determining the specific job tasks and responsibilities, the work environment, and the methods by which the tasks will be carried out to meet the goals of production.
SOCIOTECHNICAL APPROACH	The consideration of both the technology of production and the social aspects of the work environment.
JOB ENLARGEMENT	The horizontal expansion of the job to give the worker more variety, although not more responsibility. It is the reverse of specialization.
JOB ENRICHMENT	The vertical expansion of job duties to give the worker more responsibility.

Chapter 5: Work Design and Human Resource Management

SUGGESTION SYSTEM	A specific way to encourage individual participation in operations management activities.
TEAM	A small number of people with complementary skills who are committed to a common purpose, set of performance goals, and approach for which they hold themselves mutually accountable.
QUALITY CIRCLE	Small groups of employees from the same work area who meet regularly and voluntarily identify, solve, and implement solutions to work-related problems.
SELF-MANAGED TEAM	A highly trained group of employees fully responsible for turning out a well-defined segment of finished work.
GAINSHARING	An incentive program where both employees and the company share in financial gains resulting from improved productivity and profitability.

SELF-TEST QUESTIONS

MULTIPLE CHOICE

1. High-performance systems:

    A. Lead only to higher performance levels.
    B. Must be supported by education and training.
    C. Reduce flexibility and response time.
    D. Allow more rapid response by reducing flexibility.

2. The Frederick Taylor work system no longer works well because Taylor:

    A. Believed people designed and improved processes.
    B. Argued that processes must be controlled by workers.
    C. Failed to make use of the knowledge and creativity of the work force.
    D. Felt that managers must obtain the commitment of people to design, control, and improve processes.
    E. All of the above are true.

3. To motivate employees and reinforce individual and team efforts, companies can use:

   A. Monetary rewards.
   B. Training.
   C. Education.
   D. Nonmonetary rewards.
   E. All of the above are true.
   F. A, B, C but not D.

4. Workers are forced to cope with changing attitudes, new skill requirements, and increased responsibility because:

   A. If they do not, they will be forced into performing nonmechanized tasks, where pay is lower.
   B. Just a few workers can control an entire plant, reducing the number of factory jobs available.
   C. The work force today is less reliable, less dedicated, and not as competent.
   D. All of the above are true.

5. Operations managers can foster high-performance work systems by:

   A. Ensuring that human resource plans are consistent with strategic business plans.
   B. Identifying problem areas through the use of employee surveys.
   C. Work as partners with employees and other managers.
   D. All of the above are true.
   E. B and C, but not A.

6. To be an effective leader, one must:

   A. Not set high expectations.
   B. Establish a lot of rules and procedures.
   C. Motivate and encourage employees.
   D. All of the above are true.

7. Of the following statements concerning successful empowerment of employees, the one that is **NOT** true is:

   A. Employees be trained in the amount of latitude they are allowed.
   B. Information be freely shared.
   C. There be an atmosphere of trust.
   D. Managers adopt on "hands-on" leadership style.
   E. All of the above are true.

8. Job enlargement:

    A. Is a type of job specialization.
    B. Gives a worker more responsibility.
    C. Provides a worker with more variety.
    D. Is the vertical expansion of job duties.

9. Which of the following statements is **NOT** true of teams:

    A. Problem solving is more effective in groups.
    B. Teams are composed of people with similar skills who are committed to a common purpose.
    C. Teams may assume many traditional managerial functions.
    D. Teams improve employee attitudes and overall job satisfaction.
    E. All of the above are true.

10. Features of self-managed teams include:

    A. They set their own goals and inspect their own work.
    B. They share various management and leadership functions.
    C. They create their own schedules and review their performance as a group.
    D. They take responsibility for the quality of their goods and services.
    E. All of the above are true.
    F. A, B, and D but not C.

True/False

1. Human resource is the only principal resource that cannot be copied by competitors and that generates a product of greater value than the sum of its parts.

2. To develop and sustain a high-performance system, it is necessary that leadership, especially at the senior level, be very strong.

3. All businesses have three principal resources: financial, managerial, and marketing.

4. The responsibility of fostering high-performance work systems resides at the senior management level.

5. Empowerment may threaten some managers.

6. Process models describe how and why people are motivated to work.

38 PART I: FOUNDATIONS

7. A new concept, called the sociotechnical approach, considers both the technology of production and social aspects of the work environment when creating job descriptions.

8. Job enlargement gives the worker more variety without more responsibility.

9. The percentage of companies in the United States that use a suggestion system is high.

10. Both work teams and quality circles are typically composed of members from the same department or function.

FILL IN THE BLANK

1. As managers learn to work as partners with employees and other managers, traditional management is evolving toward _____.

2. _____ _____ involves determining the specific job tasks and responsibilities, the work environment, and the methods by which tasks will be carried out to meet the goals of production.

3. A team which consists mainly of managers from various functions such as sales and production that coordinate work among teams is called a _____ team.

4. _____ is an incentive program where employees and the company share in financial gains resulting from improved productivity and profitability.

5. Training strategies should be driven by _____ _____.

6. _____ can be defined as an individual's response to a felt need.

7. Theories of work motivation that have been developed by behavioral scientists can be classified as one of two types of models: _____ models and _____ models.

8. When a team performs an entire job, rather than specialized, assembly line work, they are called a _____ team.

9. The ability to produce output whose value is said to be greater than the sum of its parts is called _____.

10. _____ means giving employees authority to make decisions, gain greater control over their work, and thus more easily satisfy customers.

Chapter 5: Work Design and Human Resource Management

Key to Self-Test Questions

Multiple Choice

1. B
2. C
3. E
4. B
5. D
6. C
7. D
8. C
9. B
10. E

True/False

1. T
2. T
3. F
4. F
5. T
6. F
7. F
8. T
9. F
10. T

Fill in the Blank

1. leadership
2. Job design
3. management
4. Gainsharing
5. customer needs
6. Motivation
7. content; process
8. work
9. synergism
10. Empowerment

Chapter 6
Product Design and Development

LEARNING OBJECTIVES

Chapter 6 discusses the importance of product design and development process. The decision to develop new products is an important strategic decision that can make or break a firm in a highly competitive market. The product development process is described. Several approaches for incorporating customer needs and expectations into the design process are presented. Techniques for ensuring high quality and reliability are described. Key issues involved in designing services are discussed. Concentrate on the following:

- What are the three types of products and what are their characteristics?

- What are the advantages of standardized products?

- What are the different stages in the product development process?

- How are customer needs and wants classified?

- What are the three functions performed by research and development (R&D)?

- What is a scoring model and how is it developed and used?

- What is the usefulness of break-even analysis?

- What is prototype testing?

- What is meant by the term "Quality Function Deployment"?
- How is "value engineering" different from "value analysis"?
- What is failure-mode-and-effects (FMEA) analysis and how is it useful?
- What are the important elements in the definition of reliability?
- What is modular design and what benefits does it provide manufacturers?
- What is meant by concurrent engineering?
- How are flowcharts used in the design of services?
- Why is design for disassembly important in today's society?

Glossary

Product-Development Process	A process which describes the steps that must be taken systematically before a product can be produced and made available to the customer. It consists of idea generation, concept development, product/process development, full scale production, and finally product introduction and evaluation.
Voice of the Customer	The customer's requirements explained in their own language.
Research And Development (R&D)	The development and application of new technology to meet customer needs. R&D efforts are focused on creating a new product, extending product/or process life by improvements, and ensuring safety of the product or process for employees, users, and the environment.
Scoring Model	A screening technique based on the evaluation of the attributes of a new product. A product is ranked relative to product development, market, and financial criteria.
Nominal Specifications	Also called product parameters, they determine the functional ability and performance characteristics of the product.
Tolerances	Specify the precision required to achieve the desired performance.

Chapter 6 - Product Design and Development

Quality Function Deployment (QFD)	A philosophy and set of planning and communication tools that focus on customer requirements in coordinating the design, manufacturing, and marketing of goods.
House of Quality	A matrix used to translate customer requirements into appropriate technical requirements for each stage of product development and production.
Robust	Products that are insensitive to external sources of variation. A robust design will perform as intended even if undesirable conditions occur either in production or in the field.
Quality Engineering	The process of designing quality into a product based on a prediction of potential quality problems prior to production.
Value Engineering	A technique for reducing costs associated with product design and development. It involves cost avoidance or cost prevention before production.
Value Analysis	A technique for reducing product design and development costs. It involves cost reduction during production.
Design Reviews	Reviews designed to ensure that all the important design objectives are considered in the product development process. An attempt is made to anticipate problems before they occur, through the stimulation of discussion, the raising of questions, and the generation of new ideas and solutions to problems.
Failure Mode And Effects Analysis (FMEA)	A part of the design review process in which each component of a product is listed along with the way it may fail, the cause of failure, the effect or consequence of failure, and how it can be corrected by improving the design.
Reliability	The probability that a product, piece of equipment, or system performs its intended function for a stated period of time under specified operating conditions.
Functional Failure	Failure which occurs early in a product's life due to manufacturing or material defects.
Reliability Failure	Failure that occurs after some extended period of use. This type of failure is caused by deterioration of the product or component from a number of possible causes.
Reliability Engineering	The planning, design, manufacturing, testing, and maintenance activities necessary to achieve reliability.

RELIABILITY MANAGEMENT	The total process of establishing, achieving, and maintaining reliability objectives. It involves considerations such as: customer performance requirements, the relationships between economic factors and reliability, defining the environment and conditions in which the product will be used, etc.
REDUNDANCY	Systems that are spared by the installation of parallel components that function independently of each other.
DESIGN FOR MANUFACTURE (DFM)	A concept that ensures that product designs can be efficiently executed on the production floor. It is a way of breaking down the barriers between design and production through improved communication.
COMPUTER AIDED DESIGN (CAD)	A technology that enables a designer to interact with the computer in the design process and to eliminate time-consuming activities such as drawing blueprints and constructing prototypes.
PRODUCT SIMPLIFICATION	Reducing the complexity of a product which allows manufacturers to reduce assembly lead times and thus improve productivity, quality, flexibility, and customer response.
MODULAR DESIGN	The process of designing component parts that can be combined in a large number of ways, to increase the options available to the final consumer.
CONCURRENT ENGINEERING	The cooperative approach to product development which ensures that all departments are involved in the design process.
SIMULTANEOUS ENGINEERING	Another name for concurrent engineering.
FLOWCHART	A graphical representation used in the design of services to specify in detail the sequence of steps involved in delivering the service. It provides an excellent communication device to visualize and understand the service operation.

Chapter 6 - Product Design and Development

Self-Test Questions

Multiple Choice

1. Custom product characteristics include:

    A. Products generally made in small quantities.
    B. Products are designed to meet customer specifications.
    C. Production cost is relatively high.
    D. Customer must wait for the product.
    E. All of the above.

2. Which of the following is **NOT** an advantage of standard products?

    A. They can be mass-produced very efficiently.
    B. Their quality is generally higher.
    C. Very flexible in meeting changing customer needs.
    D. Shipments can be scheduled more frequently resulting in lower inventories.
    E. They simplify purchasing.

3. Which of the following is **NOT** one of the steps in the "new way" of product development preached by W. Edwards Deming?

    A. Design the product with appropriate tests.
    B. Make it and test it in the production line and in the laboratory.
    C. Try to sell it.
    D. Test it in service through market research.
    E. Redesign the product in light of consumer reactions to quality and price.

4. The absence of a heater in an automobile is an example of:

    A. Dissatisfier.
    B. Satisfier.
    C. Exciter.
    D. Delighter.
    E. None of the above.

5. Which of the following statements is **FALSE** regarding Research and Development (R&D)?

   A. The development and application of new technology to meet customer needs is the role of R&D.
   B. R&D efforts are focused on creating new products, extending product and/or process life, and ensuring safety.
   C. R&D is costly because it requires expensive equipment and highly qualified personnel.
   D. R&D involves high risks because for each successful project there are many failures.
   E. All of the above statements are true.

6. All of the following statements regarding services are true **EXCEPT**:

   A. The true service standard is zero defects.
   B. Quality standards take the place of the dimensions and tolerances applicable in manufacturing.
   C. Automation in service industries has resulted in more jobs and fewer new skills requirements.
   D. The core service product is a process.
   E. Services differ in their degree of customer contact and interaction, labor intensity, and customization.

7. At the concept development stage, product ideas are rejected because:

   A. Of marketing factors.
   B. They are technically infeasible.
   C. Of budgetary considerations.
   D. They are impractical to produce.
   E. All of the above.

8. Which of the following is **NOT** an important element in the definition of reliability?

   A. Probability.
   B. Quality.
   C. Performance.
   D. Operating conditions.
   E. Time.

9. A technology that enables a designer to interact with the computer in the design process and to eliminate time-consuming activities such as drawing blueprints and constructing prototypes is called:

   A. DFM
   B. QFD
   C. FMEA
   D. CAD
   E. FMS

10. Products that are insensitive to external sources of variation are called:

    A. Durable.
    B. Reliable.
    C. Robust.
    D. Superior.
    E. Environmentally safe.

TRUE/FALSE

1. Taguchi's approach to product design is to constantly direct efforts toward controlling a production process to assure consistent quality, rather than to design the product to achieve high quality.

2. Custom products are generally made in small quantities and have relatively high production cost.

3. A disadvantage of standard products is that they offer little flexibility in meeting changing customer needs.

4. R&D efforts are focused on creating a new product, extending product and/or process life, and ensuring safety of the product or process.

5. Functional failures occur after some extended period of use of the product and are usually caused by deterioration of the product or component.

6. Tolerances determine the functional ability and performance characteristics of the product.

7. Perceived quality is the difference between expected quality and actual quality.

8. Value engineering refers to cost reduction during production.

48 PART II: STRATEGIC ISSUES IN OPERATIONS

9. Techniques used to build reliability into products includes an avoidance of redundant components.

10. Concurrent engineering translates customer requirements into appropriate technical requirements for each stage of product development and production.

FILL IN THE BLANK

1. _____ products are made in large quantities, the customer has no options from which to choose, and quality is easiest to achieve because they are made the same way every time.

2. _____ are innovative features that customers would not expect, and might not even know exist, but that they like.

3. A _____ model is used to develop quantitative assessment of product success based on three criteria: product development, market, and financial.

4. _____-_____ analysis involves estimates of production costs and selling prices, and is a useful tool for estimating the economic impact of a new product.

5. _____ testing is when a model (real or simulated) is constructed to test the product's physical properties or use under actual operating conditions.

6. The term _____ _____ refers to the process of designing quality into a product based on a prediction of potential quality problems prior to production.

7. _____ is defined as the probability that a product, piece of equipment, or system performs its intended function for a stated period of time under specified operating conditions.

8. The concept of "design for disassembly" addresses environmental concerns in two ways: _____ and _____.

9. _____ _____ is a product simplification technique which allows manufactured parts and services to be combined in a large number of ways.

10. A core service product is a _____ -- that is, a method of doing things.

SELF-TEST PROBLEM

1. Lightways Computer Company has developed a new software product. This software is predicted to outperform any software product of its kind currently existing in the market. However, before adding it to its existing product line, the company wants reasonable assurance of success. Variable costs are estimated at $60 per unit produced and sold. Fixed costs are about $250,000 per year.

   A. If the selling price is set at $100, how many units must Lightways Computer Company sell to break even?

   B. Forecasted sales for the first year are 15,000 units if the price is reduced to $80. With this pricing strategy, what would be the product's contribution to profits in the first year?

KEY TO SELF-TEST QUESTIONS

MULTIPLE CHOICE

1. E   5. E   9. D
2. C   6. C   10. C
3. C   7. E
4. A   8. B

TRUE/FALSE

1. F   5. F   9. F
2. F   6. F   10. F
3. T   7. T
4. T   8. F

FILL IN THE BLANK

1. Standard
2. Exciters or Delighters
3. scoring
4. Break-even
5. Prototype
6. quality engineering
7. Reliability
8. recyclability and repairability
9. Modular design
10. process

KEY TO SELF-TEST PROBLEM

1. If we let S represent the total number of software units sold, then:

   $$Total\ Cost: TC = 250{,}000 + 60S$$

   At the selling price of $100:

   $$Total\ Revenue: TR = 100S$$

   Equating the Total Costs and Total Revenues, yields the break-even point:

   $$250{,}000 + 60S = 100S$$
   $$40S = 250{,}000$$
   $$S = 6{,}250\ Units$$

   Total Profit Contribution = Total Revenue − Total Cost:

   $$= 80(15{,}000) - [250{,}000 + 60(15{,}000)]$$

   $$= \$50{,}000$$

Chapter 7
Forecasting and Capacity Planning

LEARNING OBJECTIVES

Chapter 7 discusses the role forecasting and capacity planning in P/OM decisions. Key issues in strategic capacity planning are defined and several ways of defining and measuring capacity are presented. The use of the learning curve to estimate capacity needs is shown. Both quantitative and qualitative forecasting techniques are discussed. The appendix addresses the subject of quantitative forecasting in more detail. Concentrate on the following:

- What is the importance of forecasting in P/OM?

- What factors are used in selecting the most appropriate forecasting technique?

- How is judgmental forecasting different from statistical forecasting?

- What is strategic capacity planning?

- What issues should be considered in making strategic capacity planning decisions?

- How does the product life cycle affect capacity decisions?

- What is the difference between theoretical and demonstrated capacity?

- What is a "bottleneck" in the production process?

54 PART II: STRATEGIC ISSUES IN OPERATIONS

- ✦ What are the two ways of measuring capacity?

- ✦ What are the common strategies used for capacity expansion?

- ✦ What capacity issues are involved in facility planning?

- ✦ What factors affect the applicability of the learning curve?

- ✦ What is a time-series?

- ✦ What are the four components of a time series and how are they distinguished from one another?

- ✦ What are the different statistical forecasting techniques? How are these forecasts calculated?

- ✦ What measures are available for evaluating the accuracy of a particular forecasting method?

GLOSSARY

CAPACITY	The maximum rate of output a manufacturing or service system can produce in a particular time period.
STRATEGIC CAPACITY PLANNING	The process of determining the types and amounts of resources and production capacity required to implement an organization's strategic plan.
FORECASTING	Estimating the future demand for products/services based on historical data.
TIME-SERIES MODELS	A statistical approach that relies heavily on repeated observations, arranged in the order in which they actually occurred, to forecast future demand, recognizing both the historical trend and seasonality patterns.

LIFE-CYCLE CURVE	A graph showing changes in sales or profits against time for a new product, based on whether the product is in the introductory, growth, maturity, or decline stage.
THEORETICAL CAPACITY	The maximum output capability possible, allowing no adjustments for preventive maintenance, unplanned downtime, shutdowns, etc.
DEMONSTRATED CAPACITY	The rate of output a firm actually achieves given process limitations such as preventive maintenance, unplanned downtime, set-up time, etc.
ECONOMIES OF SCALE	Reduction in unit cost as fixed costs are spread over increasingly more units.
DISECONOMIES OF SCALE	Increase in unit cost caused by additional volume of outputs past the point of best operating level for a facility.
LEARNING CURVE	A curve showing the relationship between the number of units produced and the amount of labor required per unit.
TIME SERIES	A statistical method of forecasting based on the analysis of historical data. It makes the assumption that the past is a good indicator of the future.
TREND	A component of a time series which represents gradual shifts or movements to relatively higher or lower values over a long period of time.
CYCLICAL COMPONENT	A component of a time series representing any regular pattern or sequence of points above or below the trend line.
SEASONAL COMPONENT	A component of the time series that represents any repeating pattern or variability in the data that is less than one year in duration.
IRREGULAR COMPONENT	The component of the time series which accounts for random variability caused by short-term, unanticipated, and non-recurring factors. It is the residual variation not accounted for by the effects of trend, seasonality, or cyclicality.

FORECAST ERROR	The difference between the observed value of the time series and the forecasted value.
MEAN SQUARE ERROR (MSE)	A measure of the accuracy of a forecasting method. It is calculated as the average of the sum of the squared forecast errors.
DESEASONALIZED TIME SERIES	A time series from which the seasonal component has been removed. Seasonal indexes are used to achieve this.
MOVING AVERAGES	An average of the most recent N data values in a time series. "Moving" refers to the fact that as a new observation becomes available for the time series, the new observation replaces the oldest observation and a new moving average is computed.
EXPONENTIAL SMOOTHING	A statistical forecasting technique that uses a weighted average of past time-series values to forecast the values of the time series in the next period. An advantage of this technique is that it requires very little historical data.
SMOOTHING CONSTANT	A weight used in exponential smoothing to adjust the forecast by some fraction of the forecast error. A value between zero and one.
MEAN ABSOLUTE DEVIATION (MAD)	A measure of forecast model accuracy. It is the average of the sum of the absolute deviations for all the forecast errors. MAD is useful in tracking a forecast.

Chapter 7 - Forecasting and Capacity Planning

Self-Test Questions

Multiple Choice

1. A judgmental forecasting technique which consists of gathering judgements and opinions of key personnel based on their experience and knowledge of the situation is called:

    A. Delphi method.
    B. Market surveys.
    C. Expert opinion.
    D. Naive forecast.
    E. Time series.

2. The choice of a forecasting method depends on:

    A. The time span for which the forecast is being made.
    B. The needed frequency of forecast updating.
    C. Data requirements.
    D. The level of accuracy desired.
    E. All of the above.

3. The time series component which shows alternating patterns or sequences of points above or below the trend line is:

    A. Cyclical.
    B. Irregular.
    C. Variable.
    D. Seasonal.
    E. Trend.

4. Which of the following statements is **FALSE** about exponential smoothing?

    A. It is a statistical forecasting technique that uses a weighted average of past time-series values to forecast the value of the time series in the next period.
    B. It uses a smoothing constant, a value between zero and one, to adjust the forecast by some fraction of the forecast error.
    C. An advantage of exponential smoothing is that it requires very little historical data.
    D. If the time series is very volatile and contains substantial random variability, a small value of the smoothing constant is preferred.
    E. Smaller values of the smoothing constant have the advantage of quickly adjusting the forecasts when forecasting errors occur, allowing the forecast to react faster to changing conditions.

5. The two criteria deemed most important in determining which forecasting technique should be used are:

   A. Whether historical data is available and how reliable it is thought to be.
   B. The variable being forecast and the length of the time horizon over which the forecast is to be made.
   C. Whether the organization is a service or manufacturing organization and the availability of historical data.
   D. Whether or not an expert opinion is available, and the length of the time horizon over which the forecast is to be made.
   E. None of the above.

6. Which of the following is **NOT** true, when a product moves into the growth stage of the product life cycle?

   A. Sales volume increases and marketing's role in the corporate strategy is enhanced.
   B. Forecasting becomes a critical activity.
   C. Operations is driven by the market.
   D. Production runs are short and unit costs are high.
   E. The focus is on process innovation.

7. Setup time is an important factor in:

   A. Theoretical capacity.
   B. Demonstrated capacity.
   C. Design capacity.
   D. Strategic capacity planning.
   E. Service capacity.

8. An example of an input measure of capacity is:

   A. Barrels of oil per day.
   B. Megawatts of electricity per hour.
   C. Number of seats per flight.
   D. Number of automobiles produced per month.
   E. None of the above.

9. Capacity-planning strategy involves:

   A. An assessment of existing capacity.
   B. Forecasts of future capacity requirements.
   C. Choice of alternative ways to build capacity.
   D. Financial evaluation.
   E. All of the above.

10. Statistical methods of forecasting that are based on the analysis of historical data are called:

   A. Judgmental.
   B. Delphi.
   C. Time series.
   D. Expert opinion.
   E. None of the above.

TRUE/FALSE

1. Statistical forecasting is based on the assumption that the future will be an extrapolation of the present.

2. The Delphi method is a statistical forecasting technique that uses questionnaires, telephone contacts, or personal interviews as a means of gathering data.

3. The time span for which the forecast is being made is one of the most critical criteria in selecting a forecasting method.

4. Capacity decisions are aimed at using a corporation's resources to maximize long-term profits while meeting cash-flow requirements.

5. Capacity can be measured as the rate of output per unit of time as well as in terms of units of input.

6. Mean Square Error (MSE) is useful in tracking a forecast and is not influenced by large forecast errors.

7. The moving average is a forecasting technique that uses a weighted average of past time-series to forecast the value of the time series in the next period.

8. Theoretical capacity is the maximum output capability possible, after allowing for preventive maintenance adjustments, unplanned downtime, shutdowns, etc.

9. In service organizations, units of input is a more meaningful measure of capacity than rate of output, since the ability to meet demand depends primarily on the resources available.

10. The number of beds in a hospital is an output measure of capacity.

FILL IN THE BLANK

1. Forecasting methods can be classified as either _____ or _____.

2. When a product reaches the _____ stage in its product life cycle, demand levels off and no new distribution channels are available.

3. _____ defects do not appear during manufacturing but crop up after some period of use.

4. When several different operations are performed in sequence, the capacity of the system is determined by the _____ activity in the system.

5. _____ of _____ refers to the reduction in unit cost as fixed costs are spread over increasingly more units.

6. The measure of forecasting model accuracy calculated as the average of the sum of the absolute deviations for all the forecast errors is called _____ _____ _____.

7. When deciding to change capacity, a firm must make decisions concerning the _____, _____ and _____ of capacity additions.

8. A _____ _____ is used to show the relationship between the number of units produced and the amount of labor required per unit.

9. Because of the _____ component of a time series, forecasts are never 100 percent accurate.

10. When no historical data are available, only _____ forecasting is possible.

SELF-TEST PROBLEMS

1. A manufacturing organization is considering expanding its capacity to meet a growing demand for its products. The alternatives are to build a new plant at another location or to expand the existing plant. The economic outlook is: a 50 percent probability that the economy will remain unchanged, a 30 percent probability of an economic upturn, and a 20 percent probability of an economic downturn. Estimates of the annual returns are shown in the table below.

DECISION	ANNUAL RETURN ESTIMATES (MILLIONS)		
	ECONOMIC UPTURN	ECONOMIC DOWNTURN	ECONOMIC STABILITY
EXPAND EXISTING PLANT	$1.8	-$0.5	$0.9
BUILD NEW PLANT	$2.5	-$0.8	$1.1

   A. Use the decision tree analysis to determine the best alternative.

   B. What returns will accrue to the company if the decision in part A is followed?

2. A food packaging plant has planned shipments according to the following schedule over the next 6 weeks.

WEEK	1	2	3	4	5	6
SHIPMENTS	9500	8500	10000	8800	8200	9000

The plant normally operates two shifts per day, five days per week. During each shift 1000 food products are packaged and ready to ship.

A. Determine the theoretical capacity.

B. At what percentage of capacity is the plant actually operating?

C. Now suppose the plant stops production for 3 days due to machine breakdown, and on average 15 products are incorrectly packaged each shift. What is the demonstrated capacity for this plant?

3. A custom furniture maker has received an order to make 8 customized chairs for a dinner table. The first chair took 15 labor-hours to make. If a 90 percent learning curve is expected:

A. Determine the labor hours for the 5th chair.

B. How many labor-hours will it take to complete the order?

4. The following ticket sales information is available for the Matatu Transportation Company:

Month	Ticket Sales	Month	Ticket Sales
1	4600	13	1200
2	3900	14	600
3	2800	15	1900
4	2100	16	900
5	1400	17	1200
6	1600	18	1400
7	1400	19	1600
8	1300	20	1200
9	900	21	1300
10	1300	22	900
11	1800	23	1400
12	1500	24	1500

A. Using a 3 month and a 4 month moving average methods, forecast the ticket sales for month 25.

B. Determine the MAD values for each method.

C. Which technique would you recommend to the Matatu Company?

5. The following data shows the weekly room occupancy for Bamburi Beach Hotel & Resort for the last 3 months. The manager has decided to use the exponential smoothing technique to forecast demand for the rooms.

Week	# of	Week	# of
1	96	7	99
2	106	8	115
3	92	9	106
4	114	10	91
5	108	11	102
6	98	12	99

A. Use single exponential smoothing to forecast the demand for rooms in week 13. Use an alpha value of 0.2 and 0.6, and an initial forecast of 100 in both cases.

B. Calculate the MAD for each technique and recommend the best alternative.

Chapter 7 - Forecasting and Capacity Planning

Key to Self-Test Questions

Multiple Choice

1. C
2. E
3. A
4. E
5. B
6. D
7. B
8. C
9. E
10. C

True/False

1. F
2. F
3. T
4. T
5. T
6. F
7. F
8. F
9. T
10. F

Fill in the Blank

1. statistical, judgmental
2. maturity
3. Latent
4. bottleneck
5. Economies of scale
6. mean absolute deviation
7. amount, timing, form
8. learning curve
9. irregular
10. judgmental

Key to Self-Test Problems

1. A. The two alternatives can be evaluated by calculating the expected returns for each alternative. The results are shown below:

    Expand Existing Plant:

    $$1.8(0.3) + -0.5(0.2) + 0.9(0.5) = \$0.89 \text{ million}$$

Build New Plant:

$$2.5(0.3) + -0.8(0.2) + 1.1(0.5) = \$1.14 \; million$$

The organization should build a new plant.

 B. The expected returns from the above recommendation will be $ 1.14 million.

2. A. Theoretical capacity:

$$= (2 \; shifts/day) \; (5 \; days/week) \; (1000 \; units/shift) \; (6 \; weeks)$$
$$= 60,000 \; units \; packed$$

 B. Total shipments for next 6 weeks are 54,000 units:

$$\frac{54,000}{60,000} = 0.9$$

The plant is operating at 90 percent of the theoretical capacity over the six week period.

 C. Demonstrated capacity:

$$= [60,000 - (2 \; shifts/day) \; (1000 \; units/shift) \; (3 \; days)$$
$$- (15 \; defects/shift) \; (2 \; shifts/day) \; (27 \; days) \; \times \; 0.9$$
$$= 49,329 \; units$$

3. A. First, we must look up the unit time for the 5th unit (chair) from the learning curves table of unit values. For the 5th chair and an expected learning curve of 90 percent, this value is 0.7830.

Therefore, labor-hours for the 5th unit is:

$$15 \; \times \; 0.7830 = 11.745 \; labor-hours$$

 B. First, we must look up the total time for 8 units (chairs) from the learning curve table of cumulative values. For 8 chairs (required to complete the order) and an expected learning curve of 90 percent, this value is 6.5737.

Therefore, total labor-hours needed to complete the order is:

$$15 \; \times \; 6.5737 = 98.61 \; labor-hours$$

4. A.

Month	Ticket Sales	3-Month Moving Average	4-Month Moving Average
1	4600	-	-
2	3900	-	-
3	2800	-	-
4	2100	3766.7	-
5	1400	2933.3	3350.0
6	1600	2100.0	2550.0
7	1400	1700.0	1975.0
8	1300	1466.7	1625.0
9	900	1433.3	1425.0
10	1300	1200.0	1300.0
11	1800	1166.7	1225.0
12	1500	1333.3	1325.0
13	1200	1533.3	1375.0
14	600	1500.0	1450.0
15	1900	1100.0	1275.0
16	900	1233.3	1300.0
17	1200	1133.3	1150.0
18	1400	1333.3	1150.0
19	1600	1166.7	1350.0
20	1200	1400.0	1275.0
21	1300	1400.0	1350.0
22	900	1366.7	1375.0
23	1400	1133.3	1250.0
24	1500	1200.0	1200.0
25		1266.7	1275.0

The forecast for month 25 using the 3-month moving average is 1267 tickets. The forecast for month 25 using the 4-month moving average is 1275 tickets.

B. We can now calculate the absolute deviations and the MAD value for each method:

Month	Ticket Sales	3-Month Moving Average	Abs. Dev.	4-Month Moving Average	Abs. Dev.
1	4600	-		-	
2	3900	-		-	
3	2800	-		-	
4	2100	3766.7	1666.7	-	
5	1400	2933.3	1533.3	3350.0	1950.0
6	1600	2100.0	500.0	2550.0	950.0
7	1400	1700.0	300.0	1975.0	575.0
8	1300	1466.7	166.7	1625.0	325.0
9	900	1433.3	533.3	1425.0	525.0
10	1300	1200.0	100.0	1300.0	0.0
11	1800	1166.7	633.3	1225.0	575.0
12	1500	1333.3	166.7	1325.0	175.0
13	1200	1533.3	333.3	1375.0	175.0
14	600	1500.0	900.0	1450.0	850.0
15	1900	1100.0	800.0	1275.0	625.0
16	900	1233.3	333.3	1300.0	400.0
17	1200	1133.3	66.7	1150.0	50.0
18	1400	1333.3	66.7	1150.0	250.0
19	1600	1166.7	433.3	1350.0	250.0
20	1200	1400.0	200.0	1275.0	75.0
21	1300	1400.0	100.0	1350.0	50.0
22	900	1366.7	466.7	1375.0	475.0
23	1400	1133.3	266.7	1250.0	150.0
24	1500	1200.0	300.0	1200.0	300.0
Sum of Absolute Deviations:			9866.7		8725.0
MAD Value:			411.1		363.5

C. The 4-month moving average is a better technique for forecasting ticket sales because the MAD is smaller.

5. A. We first calculate the forecast using alpha = 0.2 and alpha = 0.6 as shown below:

WEEK	ACTUAL ROOM OCCUPANCY	FORECAST WITH ALPHA = 0.2	FORECAST WITH ALPHA = 0.6
1	96	100.0	100.0
2	106	99.2	97.6
3	92	100.6	102.6
4	114	98.9	96.2
5	108	101.9	106.9
6	98	103.1	107.6
7	99	102.1	101.8
8	115	101.5	100.1
9	106	104.2	109.0
10	91	104.6	107.2
11	102	101.9	97.5
12	99	101.9	100.2
13		101.3	99.5

The forecast for week 13 using alpha = 0.2 is:
$$F_{13} = 0.2(99) + 0.8(101.9) = 101.3$$

The forecast for week 13 using alpha = 0.6 is:
$$F_{13} = 0.6(99) + 0.4(100.2) = 99.5$$

B. We can now calculate the absolute deviations and MAD values:

Week	Actual Room Occupancy	Forecast Alpha = 0.2	Abs. Dev.	Forecast Alpha = 0.6	Abs. Dev.
1	96	100.0	4.0	100.0	4.0
2	106	99.2	6.8	97.6	8.4
3	92	100.6	8.6	102.6	10.6
4	114	98.9	15.1	96.2	17.8
5	108	101.9	6.1	106.9	1.1
6	98	103.1	5.1	107.6	9.6
7	99	102.1	3.1	101.8	2.8
8	115	101.5	13.5	100.1	14.9
9	106	104.2	1.8	109.0	3.0
10	91	104.6	13.6	107.2	16.2
11	102	101.9	0.1	97.5	4.5
12	99	101.9	2.9	100.2	1.2
Sum of Absolute Deviations:			80.7		94.1
MAD Value:			6.73		7.84

The exponential smoothing technique using alpha = 0.2 is better because the MAD is smaller.

Chapter 8
Facility Location and Distribution System Design

LEARNING OBJECTIVES

Chapter 8 addresses the basic concepts involved in determining appropriate locations for new facilities such as plants and warehouses. Sound location decision making is very critical because large amounts of capital investment is required and, once built, the facility cannot easily be moved. The various factors involved in selecting a location are discussed. The use of "scoring" models to assist in location decision is illustrated. Quantitative models such as the "center-of-gravity" method and the "transportation" model are introduced. Factors affecting service-facility location decisions are described. Concentrate on the following:

- How are facility location decisions important in meeting strategic objectives?

- What does the term <u>business logistics</u> mean? What are the key elements of a logistics system?

- What is the principal goal of a logistics system?

- How is a "push" distribution system different from a "pull" distribution system?

- How does one determine the best overall distribution strategy?

- What are the major economic and non-economic factors that influence location decisions?

- What is the most commonly used method for evaluating non-economic factors in a facility location study? What are the advantages and disadvantages of this method?

- What role does a warehouse or distribution center play with respect to total distribution design?

- What cost tradeoffs occur when the number of distribution centers increases?

- How does the center-of-gravity method work? What assumption is made when using this method?

- What are the benefits of using computerized systems for making location and distribution decisions?

- How are location decisions made for service facilities different from those made for manufacturing organizations?

- What are the major location decisions factors for retail, public-service and, emergency facilities?

GLOSSARY

BUSINESS LOGISTICS The management of all activities that facilitate product flow to the point of final consumption as well as the information flows that are necessary to provide adequate levels of customer service at reasonable costs.

CROSS-DOCKING A process by which products are unloaded from plant shipments, staged on the docks (but not sent to storage), and quickly reloaded for shipment to individual customers. Usually facilitated by distribution centers that are under a "pull" system of production.

CONSOLIDATION The collecting together of individual orders through the use of a warehouse as a central location (as opposed to shipping small quantities of each product directly from the plant to retail stores).

CENTER-OF-GRAVITY A method for determining the location for a single warehouse.

CHAPTER 8 - FACILITY LOCATION AND DISTRIBUTION SYSTEM DESIGN

METHOD	The center of gravity is defined as the location that minimizes the weighted distance between the warehouse and its supply and distribution points, with the distance weighted by the volume supplied or consumed.
TRANSPORTATION PROBLEM	A linear programming technique used to find the minimal cost of shipping products from several sources to several destinations.

SELF-TEST QUESTIONS

MULTIPLE CHOICE

1. The key elements of a logistics system are:

   A. Purchasing, transportation, and shipping.
   B. Purchasing, receiving, and shipping.
   C. Distribution, ordering, and storing.
   D. Transportation, inventory, and order processing.
   E. None of the above.

2. To determine the best overall distribution strategy, a firm must consider:

   A. Transportation costs and methods.
   B. Inventory costs.
   C. Storage requirements.
   D. Sales trends and projected growth.
   E. All of the above.

3. Land costs, proximity to transportation systems, utilities, and zoning restrictions are among the important factors to be considered in a:

   A. Regional decision.
   B. Site decision.
   C. Construction decision.
   D. Community decision.
   E. Local decision.

4. The center-of-gravity method takes into account all of these **EXCEPT**:

   A. The distance from a competitors warehouse.
   B. The location of markets.
   C. The volume of goods moved.
   D. The transportation costs.
   E. The location of plants.

5. For emergency services such as fire protection and police, a principal criterion for location decision is:

   A. Visibility of site from highways.
   B. Traffic volume around the site.
   C. Location of competitors.
   D. Response time.
   E. Road access.

6. A special purpose algorithm that can be used to determine the minimum cost transportation plan between multiple supply and destination locations is:

   A. Locational cost-volume analysis.
   B. Transportation problem.
   C. Heuristics.
   D. Center-of-gravity method.
   E. Scoring model.

7. Which of the following is **NOT** a global distribution issue?

   A. Customs.
   B. Packaging.
   C. Taxes.
   D. Time zones.
   E. Tariffs and other trade restrictions.

8. In evaluating the level of customer service provided by distribution centers, two measures commonly used depend on the number and location of warehouses. These two measures are:

   A. The average order processing time and the percentage of shipments delivered on time.
   B. The percentage of shipments delivered on time and the percentage of orders that are accurately filled.
   C. The percentage of orders that are accurately filled and the number of damaged items.
   D. The number of damaged items and the average order processing times.
   E. None of the above.

9. Which of the following is **NOT** an example of a public-service facility?

   A. Post offices.
   B. Schools.
   C. ATM machines.
   D. Highways.
   E. Parks.

10. Which of the following statements is **NOT** true regarding service facility location:

    A. Service facility location problems often involve multiple sites.
    B. Service facilities are the terminal points in the system, the points where demand takes place.
    C. Service facilities generally serve a small geographic area.
    D. Service systems do not have the traditional product-distribution channel structures characteristic of manufacturing systems.
    E. The criteria for choosing service facility locations is the same as those used in manufacturing.

TRUE/FALSE

1. The principal goal of a logistics system is to provide customers with an accurate and quick response to their orders at the lowest possible cost.

2. An inaccurate sales forecast in a "pull" system leads to increased inventory, larger distribution centers, and higher stock-transfer costs.

3. Location decisions are based on economic factors only.

4. Warehouses and distribution centers allow a company to store finished goods for efficient distribution to points of use.

5. The center-of-gravity method is based on the assumption that transportation rates to and from the warehouse are equal.

6. Pull systems work best when sales patterns are consistent and when there is a small number of distribution centers and products.

7. Location decisions are made by selecting a region, community then site.

8. As the number of distribution centers increases, total transportation costs generally also increase.

76 PART II: STRATEGIC ISSUES IN OPERATIONS

9. Two drawbacks in using the transportation model alone are that it assumes that facility locations are fixed and does not consider location and transportation simultaneously.

10. A major problem in locating public-service facilities is the lack of easily quantifiable data.

FILL IN THE BLANK

1. _____ _____ is a process by which products are unloaded from plant shipments, staged on the docks, and quickly reloaded for shipment to individual customers.

2. The most common method for evaluating non-economic factors in a facility-location study is _____ _____.

3. The location that minimizes the weighted distance between the warehouse and its supply and distribution points, with the distance weighted by the volume supplied or consumed is called _____-_____-_____.

4. _____ cost is the cost of manufacturing, warehousing, and transportation.

5. The optimum number of distribution centers will balance transportation costs with _____ and _____ costs.

6. Computer-based distribution and location planning has received a boost from recent developments in _____ _____ _____ technology.

7. In locating facilities that are oriented toward sales, the principal factors are market-related and the important data are _____.

8. _____ _____ refers to the management of all activities that facilitate product and information flow necessary to provide adequate levels of customer service at reasonable costs.

9. A _____ decision involves the selection of a particular location within the chosen community.

10. Customer service is often measured by the average _____-_____ time.

CHAPTER 8 - FACILITY LOCATION AND DISTRIBUTION SYSTEM DESIGN

SELF-TEST PROBLEMS

1. Blockmeister Video is trying to evaluate three alternative sites for its new store location. The company has collected the following information concerning where to locate the new store:

CRITERIA	WEIGHT	LOCATION		
		A	B	C
Residential Density	0.4	80	60	90
Highway Accessibility	0.3	50	90	70
Land & Contruct. Cost	0.2	70	60	80
Property Taxes	0.1	50	40	40

   Use the scoring model method to select the best location site.

2. Tusker Beer Company is attempting to locate a distribution warehouse for its beer products somewhere in Texas. The warehouse will ship to four major centers of market demand: Dallas, Houston, San Antonio, and Austin. Information on the average monthly demand volumes and the coordinate locations of the four demand centers is shown in the table below. Using the center-of-gravity method, determine the best location for the warehouse.

LOCATION	X-COORDINATE	Y-COORDINATE	MONTHLY DEMAND
Dallas	130	140	3000
Houston	160	50	5000
San Antonio	100	85	3000
Austin	115	100	1500

CHAPTER 8 - FACILITY LOCATION AND DISTRIBUTION SYSTEM DESIGN

KEY TO SELF-TEST QUESTIONS

MULTIPLE CHOICE

1. D
2. E
3. B
4. A
5. D
6. B
7. C
8. A
9. C
10. E

TRUE/FALSE

1. T
2. F
3. F
4. T
5. T
6. F
7. T
8. F
9. T
10. T

FILL IN THE BLANK

1. Cross docking
2. scoring model
3. center-of-gravity
4. Delivered
5. inventory, order-processing
6. geographic information system
7. demographic
8. Business logistics
9. site
10. order-processing

KEY TO SELF-TEST PROBLEMS

1. Using the "scoring" model, the following scores are obtained:

   $Location\ A$: $80(0.4) + 50(0.3) + 70(0.2) + 50(0.1) = 66$
   $Location\ B$: $60(0.4) + 90(0.3) + 60(0.2) + 40(0.1) = 67$
   $Location\ C$: $90(0.4) + 70(0.3) + 80(0.2) + 40(0.1) = 77$

   Hence, location B appears to be the best location.

2. The coordinates for the center of gravity are:

$$Cx = \frac{130(3000) + 160(5000) + 100(3000) + 115(1500)}{3000 + 5000 + 3000 + 1500} = 133$$

$$Cy = \frac{140(3000) + 50(5000) + 85(3000) + 100(1500)}{3000 + 5000 + 3000 + 1500} = 86$$

The center of gravity mark is shown in the plot below. The company should find a site close to that mark to locate their warehouse.

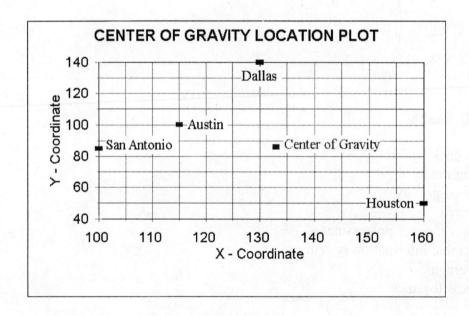

Chapter 9
Process Technology and Design

LEARNING OBJECTIVES

*C*hapter 9 introduces process technology and automation and their strategic importance to organizations. The choice of technology affects a firm's ability to manufacture products that meet the customers' requirements and the firm's strategic goals of quality, flexibility, dependability, and cost. Key elements of modern automation are reviewed and several manufacturing automation systems are also described. The steps involved in designing production processes is discussed and different types of work measurement techniques are presented. Concentrate on the following:

- ✦ What is process technology?

- ✦ How is make-to-order different from make-to-stock production system?

- ✦ What is the differences in continuous flow, mass-production, batch, job shop, and project processes?

- ✦ What is the difference in manual, mechanized, and automated process technology?

- ✦ What is a product-process matrix and what information does it provide to operations managers?

- ✦ What is an NC machine? How is it different from a CNC machine?

82 PART III: DESIGNING AND MANAGING PRODUCTION PROCESSES

- What is a robot and what are some of the benefits of using robots?

- What are some of the applications of machine vision systems in production?

- How have information based technologies improved productivity and quality?

- What is the differences among CAD/CAE, CAM, FMS, and CIMS?

- How has automation impacted manufacturing and service organizations? What has been the impact of automation on the labor force?

- What are the various steps involved in process planning and design?

- What is an assembly chart, a flow process chart, and a multiple-activity chart?

- What is an operation chart and how can it be used to improve work methods?

- What is a time standard?

- What are the different types of work measurement techniques? What are these techniques used for in organizations?

GLOSSARY

PROCESS	A specific combination of machines, operators, work methods, materials, tools, and environmental factors that together convert inputs to outputs.
PROCESS TECHNOLOGY	The methods and equipment used to manufacture a product or deliver a service. An essential component of an organization's operations strategy.
HARD TECHNOLOGY	Involves the application of computers, sensors, robots, and other mechanical and electronic aids in the manufacture of a product or delivery of a service.

SOFT TECHNOLOGY	Refers to the application of computer software and other techniques that support manufacturing and service organizations. Examples include office automation software and database management systems.
PRODUCT-PROCESS MATRIX	Represents the interaction of product and process structure. The diagonal of the matrix shows typical matchings of products and processes. Moving down the diagonal, the emphasis in both product and process structure shifts from high flexibility to low cost.
AUTOMATION	The use of machines to provide both power and control over the production process. It is making the work environment more comfortable for workers and freeing them from onerous and dangerous jobs. It also enables firms to improve productivity and quality, and increase flexibility.
NUMERICALLY CONTROLLED (NC)	Machine tools which enable machinist's skills to be duplicated by a computer program that is stored on a computer medium. The computer program controls the movements of a tool used to make complex shapes.
COMPUTER NUMERICAL CONTROL (CNC)	The machine is controlled by a small computer. These computer systems can prepare detailed instructions automatically if the part shape, tools required, and machining information are provided.
ROBOT	A programmable machine designed to handle materials or tools in the performance of a variety of tasks. They consist of two major components: a manipulator, much like a human arm and wrist that carries a tool to perform work, and a control system to provide the guidance to direct the manipulator to follow a prescribed sequence of operations.
MACHINE VISION SYSTEMS	Devices that automatically receive and interpret an image of a real scene to obtain information and/or control machines or processes. They consist of a camera and video analyzer, a microcomputer, and a display screen.
BAR-CODE TECHNOLOGY	An optical scanner used to read product bar codes. Some benefits include faster processing, reduced errors, less paperwork, less time spent replenishing inventories, and reduced customer waiting time.
ELECTRONIC DATA INTERCHANGE	Integrated system in which computers in one organization exchange information directly with computers in another organization.

COMPUTER-AIDED DESIGN / COMPUTER-AIDED ENGINEERING (CAD/CAE)	Enables engineers to design, analyze, test, and "manufacture" products before they physically exist. It also allows for storage and retrieval of designs for easy updating and automatic creation of bills of materials and process information for production-planning and scheduling systems.
FLEXIBLE MANUFACTURING SYSTEMS (FMS)	A logical extension of CAM. This system consists of two or more computer-controlled machines linked by automated handling devices such as robots and transport systems. Computers direct the overall sequence of operations and route the workpiece to the appropriate machine, select and load the proper tools, and control the operations performed by the machine.
COMPUTER-ASSISTED MANUFACTURING (CAM)	Involves computer control of the manufacturing process, such as determining tool movements and cutting speeds.
COMPUTER-INTEGRATED MANUFACTURING (CIM)	An integration of CAD, CAM, and FMS. These systems represent the union of hardware, software, database management, and communications to plan and control production activities from planning and design to manufacturing and distribution.
BILL OF MATERIALS (BOM)	A record that shows the list of the items in the product structure, their level of assembly, and the quantity required to produce one unit of a product, or end item.
ASSEMBLY CHART	A graphical representation of the order of assembly for a product.
FLOW-PROCESS CHART	Provides more detailed information about a production process. It describes the specific sequence of operations, transportations, inspections, storages, and delays of a production process.
WORK CENTER	Consists of one or more people and/or machines that can be considered as one unit for the purposes of performing work tasks.
OPERATION CHART	Often used to describe a manual task. Individual motions of the right hand and the left hand are applied to operations, transportations, inspections, storages, and delays.

CHAPTER 9: PROCESS TECHNOLOGY AND DESIGN

MULTIPLE-ACTIVITY CHART	A tool used to design methods for worker-machine interaction. The activities of each component of a system, such as machines and people, are graphically represented along a vertical time scale.
WORK MEASUREMENT	A useful tool for evaluating alternative process designs for labor-intensive work. Its purpose is to develop time standards for the performance of jobs.
TIME STANDARD	The amount of time a trained operator working at a normal pace and using a prescribed method takes to perform a task.
TIME STUDY	One of the several techniques for work measurement. It is the development of a time standard by observing a task and analyzing it with the use of a stop watch.
WORK SAMPLING	A method of randomly observing work over a period of time to obtain a distribution of the activities of an individual or a group of employees. It can be used to determine the percentage of idle time for people or machines in a job.

SELF-TEST QUESTIONS

MULTIPLE CHOICE

1. An example of information based technology is:
   A. Electronic data interchange.
   B. Flexible manufacturing systems.
   C. Computer aided design.
   D. Programmable automation.
   E. Robotics.

PART III: DESIGNING AND MANAGING PRODUCTION PROCESSES

2. Which of the following is a narrow corporate view of process technology?

   A. Manufacturing technology is an integrated activity that cuts across functional boundaries and is continuous over time.
   B. Technology is a set of general capabilities that meet the firm's current needs as well as future product market strategies.
   C. Technical knowledge is in the domain of the specialist and is neither required nor useful to general managers.
   D. Improvement comes from incremental efforts that are difficult for competitors to imitate.
   E. Technology is a product of holistic decision making that includes a variety of subjective elements, nonfinancial and financial and long-term as well as short term.

3. Continuous flow production processes are characterized by:

   A. High production volume.
   B. High degree of product standardization.
   C. Low unit costs.
   D. Use of highly specialized equipment.
   E. All of the above.

4. Firms that operate below the diagonal on the product-process matrix have:

   A. Greater flexibility and lower cost.
   B. Less flexibility and lower cost.
   C. Greater flexibility and higher cost.
   D. Less flexibility and higher cost.
   E. None of the above.

5. Which of the following statements is **FALSE** regarding automation?

   A. Automation is the use of machines to provide both power and control over the production process.
   B. Automation enables firms to improve productivity and quality.
   C. Automation is making the work environment more comfortable for workers.
   D. Automation reduces a firms flexibility to respond rapidly to changing demands.
   E. Automation frees workers from onerous and dangerous jobs.

6. An example of machine vision systems application in production is:

   A. Security.
   B. Inventory control.
   C. Quality control.
   D. Process mapping.
   E. Filing.

CHAPTER 9: PROCESS TECHNOLOGY AND DESIGN 87

7. Which of the following is **NOT** an advantage of using machines for work?

   A. Machines provide precise, accurate, and fast responses.
   B. Machines are highly reliable for routine tasks.
   C. Machines can perform tasks beyond human capabilities.
   D. Machines can store and process large amounts of information.
   E. Machines can improvise and adapt to new situations.

8. If a stopwatch is used to develop a standard through observation and analysis of a task, then the technique being employed for work measurement is:

   A. Historical time data.
   B. Time study.
   C. Predetermined motion-time data.
   D. Standard data.
   E. Work sampling.

9. Which of the following statements is **NOT** true regarding the product-process matrix.

   A. By positioning a business off the diagonal of the product-process matrix, a company can differentiate itself from its competitors.
   B. Movement to the right of the diagonal makes it increasingly difficult to coordinate production and marketing.
   C. With movement to the left of the diagonal, profitability may suffer, since volume remains small but equipment costs increase.
   D. Moving down the diagonal of the product-process matrix, the emphasis in both product and process structure shifts form high flexibility to low cost.
   E. All of the above statements are true.

10. Automation is:

    A. The use of machines to provide both power and control over the production process.
    B. The process by which scientific knowledge is applied in the work place.
    C. The use of computers to program, direct, and control production equipment.
    D. The formal process by which integration of organizational functions may be achieved.
    E. None of the above.

TRUE/FALSE

1. Hard technology refers to the application of computer software and other techniques that support manufacturing and service organizations. F

88 PART III: DESIGNING AND MANAGING PRODUCTION PROCESSES

2. Production systems can usually be classified into one of two categories: make-to-order and make-to-stock. T

3. An operation chart is a flow-process chart of the motion of the left hand and the right hand and is used to help design work methods. F

4. Hayes and Wheelwright suggest that a broad corporate view of process technology may be the source of many strategic problems that have surfaced in U.S. manufacturing firms. F

5. Continuous-flow production processes are used for high volume production of discrete units. T

6. Make-to-order and make-to-stock systems differ with respect to the variety and quantity of products made. T

7. Moving down the diagonal of the product-process matrix, the emphasis in both product and process structure shifts form high cost to low flexibility. False T

8. Work measurement is a method of randomly observing work over a period of time to obtain a distribution of the activities of an individual or a group of employees. F

9. A bill of materials consists of the items in the product structure, their level of assembly, and the quantity required for each parent item. T

10. Flexible Manufacturing Systems consist of two or more computer-controlled machines linked by automated handling devices such as robots and transport systems. T

FILL IN THE BLANK

1. _____ technology utilizes machines that are under human control.

2. A _____ is a programmable machine designed to handle materials or tools in the performance of a variety of tasks. It consists of two major components: a manipulator and a control system.

3. _Computer_ _Integrated_ _Manufacturing_ is a complete integration of CAD/CAE, CAM, and FMS. It represents the union of hardware, software, database management, and communications to plan and control production activities from planning and design to manufacturing and distribution.

CHAPTER 9: PROCESS TECHNOLOGY AND DESIGN   89

4. A __work__ __center__ consists of one or more people and/or machines that can be considered as one unit for the purpose of performing work tasks.

5. Two tools that facilitate the design of work methods are __operation__ charts and __multiple__ - __activity__ charts.

6. A __time__ __standard__ is generally defined as the amount of time a trained operator working at a normal pace and using a prescribed method takes to perform a task.

7. __Machine__ __Vision__ systems automatically receive and interpret an image of a real scene to obtain information and/or control machines or processes.

8. A work measurement technique that develops time standards by observing a task and analyzing it with the use of a stop watch is __time study__.

9. A __Process__ is a specific combination of machines, operators, work methods, materials, tools, and environmental factors that together convert inputs to outputs.

10. The configuration of a production process where all materials, workers, etc. are brought to the site and the output delivered is large, unique, and complex is __project__.

90 PART III: DESIGNING AND MANAGING PRODUCTION PROCESSES

SELF-TEST PROBLEMS

1. Which system has the highest reliability?

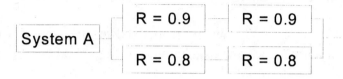

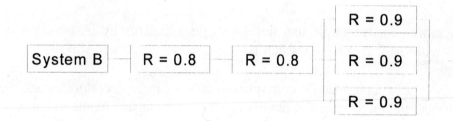

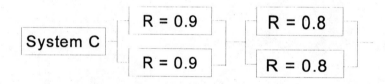

2. Twiga Car Rental Service has attempted to streamline the process of renting cars so that customers may obtain cars with minimum delay. The manager has timed 40 transactions from the time the agent begins talking with the customer until the customer is handed the keys and a completed contract. If the estimated standard deviation is 2.79 minutes, how many observations are required to estimate the mean time with 95 percent confidence within an accuracy of 0.5 minute?

Key to Self-Test Questions

Multiple Choice

1. A
2. C
3. E
4. B
5. D
6. C
7. E
8. B
9. E
10. A

True/False

1. F
2. T
3. T
4. F
5. F
6. T
7. F
8. F
9. T
10. T

Fill in the Blank

1. Mechanized
2. robot
3. Computer Integrated Manufacturing
4. work center
5. operation, multiple-activity
6. time standard
7. Machine vision
8. time study
9. process
10. project

Key to Self-Test Problems

1. **System A**:

    First, calculate the reliability of the two legs as:

    $$0.9 \times 0.9 = 0.81$$
    $$0.8 \times 0.8 = 0.64$$

    Reliability of the system is:

    $$= 1 - (1 - 0.81)(1 - 0.64) = 0.932$$

System B:

First, solve for the reliability of the "spared" section:

$$1 - (1 - 0.9)(1 - 0.9)(1 - 0.9) = 0.999$$

Reliability of the system is:

$$= 0.8 \times 0.8 \times 0.999 = 0.639$$

System C:

First calculate the reliability of each "spared" section:

$$1 - (1 - 0.9)(1 - 0.9) = 0.99$$
$$1 - (1 - 0.8)(1 - 0.8) = 0.96$$

Reliability of the system is:

$$= 0.99 \times 0.96 = 0.95$$

Therefore, System C is the most reliable.

2. We first need to determine the Z value from the standard normal distribution table.

   For a 95 percent confidence, $Z = 1.96$

   We can now calculate the number of observations:

   $$n = \frac{(z)^2 \sigma^2}{E^2} = \frac{(1.96)^2 (2.79)^2}{(0.5)^2} = 120$$

Chapter 10
Facility Layout and Workplace Design

LEARNING OBJECTIVES

Chapter 10 focuses on the strategic importance of facility layout and workplace design. Good facility layout and workplace design add value to an organization's products and services. Some benefits include productivity improvements, reduced costs of handling and carrying work-in-process inventory, effective utilization of space, and improved employee morale. Major types of facility layouts are discussed with circumstances that would justify their use. Various approaches for designing facility layouts are introduced. The chapter ends with a discussion of the design of individual workplaces, with a particular emphasis on human factors that must be considered in promoting a safe and healthful work environment. Concentrate on the following:

- What are the objectives of facility layout studies?

- What conditions must exist for facility layout studies to be conducted?

- What are the four major types of layout patterns? What are the advantages and disadvantages of each?

- What factors are important when making facility layout decisions for service organizations?

- What are the most commonly used materials handling-systems in manufacturing?

- How is conveyor paced production lines different from unpaced production lines?

96 PART III: DESIGNING AND MANAGING PRODUCTION PROCESSES

- ✦ What is meant by cycle time, and why is it important? How is line efficiency measured?

- ✦ What is the major criterion in designing new layouts?

- ✦ What are the three basic steps involved in the design of group layout? What criteria can be used in the design of group layouts?

- ✦ What questions are addressed when designing a workplace for an individual worker?

- ✦ What do ergonomists do?

- ✦ When designing individual workplaces, what environmental factors are considered? How does OSHA influence these decisions?

GLOSSARY

PRODUCT LAYOUT	Equipment arrangement is based on the sequence of operations performed in production, and products move in a continuous path from one department to the next. Continuous flow, mass production, and batch processing production processes are usually arranged in this way.
PROCESS LAYOUT	A functional grouping of machines or activities that do similar work. Job shops are an example of firms that use process layouts.
GROUP TECHNOLOGY	Also called cellular manufacturing, it is the classification of parts into families so that efficient mass-production-type layouts can be designed for families of parts.
GROUP (CELLULAR) LAYOUT	A process layout designed by grouping together different machines (called cells) needed for producing families of parts.
FIXED-POSITION LAYOUT	A layout used for the construction of large items such as heavy machine tools, airplanes, locomotives, etc. It requires tools and components to be brought to one place for assembly.

Chapter 10: Facility Layout and Workplace Design

MATERIALS HANDLING	The movement of materials through the different phases of the production process. A specific materials handling equipment can be selected once one knows what needs to be moved and where it has to go.
PRODUCTION LINE	A fixed sequence of production stages, each consisting of one or more machines or workstations.
FLOW-BLOCKING DELAY	One of two sources of delay in unpaced production lines. This delay occurs when a work center completes a unit but cannot release it because the in-process storage at the next stage is full.
LACK-OF-WORK DELAY	One of two sources of delay in unpaced production lines. This delay occurs whenever one stage completes work and no units from the previous stage are awaiting processing.
CYCLE TIME	The interval between successive parts coming off the assembly line.
LOAD MATRIX	Lists the number of moves from one department to another over some time period, such as one year. Useful in determining which departments should be placed close to each other in order to minimize materials handling costs.
CRAFT	(Computerized Relative Allocation of Facilities Technique). One of the most widely used computerized facility-layout programs. The technique attempts to minimize the total materials handling cost for a particular layout.
ERGONOMICS	The designing of workplaces, tools, instruments, etc. that take into account the physical capabilities of people. It attempts to improve worker productivity and workplace safety.
CUMULATIVE TRAUMA DISORDER (CTD)	Injuries such as lower back pain, carpal tunnel syndrome, tennis elbow, and other forms of tendinitis. Typically caused by mismatching human physical abilities and task-performance requirements.

98 PART III: DESIGNING AND MANAGING PRODUCTION PROCESSES

SELF-TEST QUESTIONS

MULTIPLE CHOICE

1. Which of the following is **NOT** a layout pattern commonly used in designing production processes?

   A. Team layout.
   B. Group layout.
   C. Product layout.
   D. Process layout.
   E. Fixed position layout.

2. Product layouts:

   A. Consist of a functional grouping of machines or activities that do similar work.
   B. Can lead to increased worker satisfaction because of the inherent diversity of jobs.
   C. Arrange equipment based on the sequence of operations performed in production.
   D. Often require that products be moved frequently between departments.
   E. Are not described by any of the above statements.

3. Which of the following is **NOT** a disadvantage associated with product layouts?

   A. A breakdown in one machine can cause an entire production line to shut down.
   B. Flexibility is limited since the layout is determined by the product.
   C. Capacity of the production line is determined by the bottleneck work center.
   D. The high level of division of labor provides little job satisfaction.
   E. Higher in-process inventory, since jobs from several departments may arrive and wait at a particular department.

4. All of these are common types of materials handling-systems **EXCEPT**:

   A. Industrial trucks.
   B. Pulleys.
   C. Automated storage and retrieval systems.
   D. Fixed-path conveyor systems.
   E. Overhead cranes.

CHAPTER 10: FACILITY LAYOUT AND WORKPLACE DESIGN 99

5. The purpose of facility layout studies is:

    A. To minimize delays in materials handling.
    B. To maintain flexibility.
    C. To use labor and space effectively.
    D. To promote high employee morale.
    E. All of the above.

6. Unpaced production lines:

    A. Are more appropriate than conveyor-paced lines when there is a low variance in times required to perform individual operations.
    B. Provide no worker control, are monotonous, and offer little social interaction.
    C. Provide no buffers between successive operations.
    D. Have two sources of delay: flow-blocking delay, and lack of work delay.
    E. Are not described by any of the above statements.

7. Which of the following statements is **NOT** true about ergonomics?

    A. Ergonomic studies attempt to increase productivity at the expense of workplace safety.
    B. Ergonomic studies and proper design of the workplace can reduce or eliminate cumulative trauma disorders.
    C. Ergonomics is good business and can increase the productivity of the organization.
    D. Ergonomics is also referred to as human factors engineering.
    E. Ergonomics draws information from disciplines such as anthropology and work physiology.

8. If such factors as height, arm length, and range of visual capability are being considered, then ergonomics is drawing information from the discipline of:

    A. Biomechanics.
    B. Physical anthropology.
    C. Work physiology.
    D. Historical sociology.
    E. None of the above.

9. An example of a product layout configuration would be:

    A. Auto production.
    B. Building a bridge.
    C. Customized furniture production.
    D. Gourmet restaurant.
    E. Ship building.

10. The configuration for operations characterized by a functional grouping of machines or activities that do similar work is:
    A. Product layout.
    B. Group layout.
    C. Job shop.
    D. Batch processing.
    E. Fixed position layout.

TRUE/FALSE

1. In service organizations the basic trade-off between product and process layouts is flexibility versus productivity.

2. Fixed position layout involves construction of large items and requires tools and components to be brought to one place for assembly.

3. Automated guided vehicles (AGVs) are high technology materials handling or storage configurations that usually involve computer control, unit loads, and digital computer interface/control.

4. In an unpaced production line, a flow-blocking delay occurs whenever one stage completes work and no units from the previous stage are awaiting processing.

5. A group or cellular layout consists of a functional grouping of machines or activities that do similar work.

6. Conveyor systems are generally used when the route does not vary, continuous movement is required, and automatic sorting, in-process inspection, or in-process storage is required.

7. Industrial safety is a function of the job, the human operator, and the surrounding environment.

8. When a production process uses a product layout, the capacity of the production line is determined by the bottleneck work center.

9. A disadvantage of process layout configuration is low employee morale due to little job satisfaction.

10. Conveyor paced assembly lines are commonly used for manual assembly tasks.

CHAPTER 10: FACILITY LAYOUT AND WORKPLACE DESIGN

FILL IN THE BLANK

1. _____ refers to the specific arrangement of physical facilities.

2. _Automated Guided Vehicles_ are computer-controlled, driverless vehicles guided by wires embedded in the shop floor.

3. A _Production Line_ is a fixed sequence of production stages, each consisting of one or more machines or workstations.

4. A _Load Matrix_ lists the number of moves from one department to another over some period of time, such as one year.

5. _Ergonomics_ is concerned with improving productivity and safety by designing workplaces, tools, instruments, and so on, that take into account the physical capabilities of people.

6. The three key safety issues that relate to the surrounding environment are _lighting_, _Temp + Humid_, and _Noise_.

7. The assigned location where a worker performs his or her job is called a _workstation_.

8. The _cycle_ time is the interval between successive parts coming off the assembly line.

9. A major design consideration for production lines is the assignment of operations so that all stages are more or less equally loaded, or _balanced_.

10. _Group Technology_ is the classification of parts into families so that efficient mass-production-type layouts can be designed for families of parts.

SELF-TEST PROBLEMS

1. The assembly of an air conditioning unit requires the following tasks:

TASK	A	B	C	D	E	F	G	H
TIME (MINUTES)	2	6	3	4	5	4	2	4

The efficiency is 90%, the work week is 40 hours, and the desired number of units is 180 per week. Assuming that the tasks are performed in the sequence as listed above:

   A. Determine the cycle time.

   B. How many work stations would be required?

   C. Determine the line efficiency?

2. Now suppose *Problem 1* above was modified to include predecessor relationships between tasks as shown below:

Task	A	B	C	D	E	F	G	H
Time (Minutes)	2	6	3	4	5	4	2	4
Predecessor	-	A	B	B	B	A	D,E	C,F,G

A. Draw a precedence diagram.

B. If the assembly line must produce 50 air conditioning units per day, calculate the cycle time. Assume an 8 hour work day.

C. Balance the line using the longest task rule to assign tasks to workstations.

D. Determine the line efficiency.

104 PART III: DESIGNING AND MANAGING PRODUCTION PROCESSES

KEY TO SELF-TEST QUESTIONS

MULTIPLE CHOICE

1. A
2. C
3. E
4. B
5. E
6. D
7. A
8. B
9. A
10. C

TRUE/FALSE

1. F
2. T
3. F
4. F
5. F
6. T
7. T
8. T
9. F
10. T

FILL IN THE BLANK

1. Facility layout
2. Automated guided vehicles
3. production line
4. load matrix
5. Ergonomics
6. lighting, temperature & humidity, and noise
7. workstation
8. cycle
9. balanced
10. Group technology

KEY TO SELF-TEST PROBLEMS

1. For a desired output rate of 180 units per week, 36 units must be produced each day.

   At 90% efficiency, (0.9)(8 hours/day) = 7.2 productive hours available.

   The cycle time is:

   $$C = \frac{(7.2 \ hours/day)(60 \ minutes/hour)}{36 \ units/day} = 12 \ minutes/unit$$

We can now group the tasks to minimize efficiency:

A,B,C	D,E	F,G,H
2,6,3	4,5	4,2,4

The line efficiency is:

$$= \frac{Sum\ of\ all\ Operation\ Times}{(Cycle\ Time)(No.\ of\ Stations)} = \frac{30\ minutes}{(12\ minutes/unit)(3)} = 83.3\%$$

2. The first step is to draw the precedence diagram:

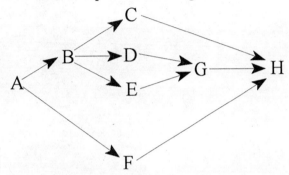

For an output rate of 50 units a day, with (8 hours)(60 minutes/hour) = 480 minutes available, the cycle time is:

$$C = \frac{480\ minutes/day}{50\ units/day} = 10\ minutes/unit$$

Now we balance the line, using the "largest time first" rule to assign tasks to stations.

STATION			
1	2	3	4
A,B	E,F	D,C,G	H
2,6	5,4	4,3,2	4

The line efficiency is:

$$\frac{30\ minutes}{10\ minutes/unit)(4)} = 75\%$$

Chapter 11
Process Management

LEARNING OBJECTIVES

***C**hapter 11* introduces process management and explains its focus and its goals. Also addressed are the strategies for process management and improvement. As these strategies are examined, the concept of control and its role in quality is discussed, as well as techniques for preventing defects. The philosophy of continuous improvement and tools for the improvement process are explained. As you read this chapter, focus on the following:

- What is process control?

- What is the function of quality control? What are its objectives?

- In a quality control system, why would you be concerned with inspection and measurement? What are the types of measurement? How is inspection quantity and location determined?

- What are the different techniques for quality control?

- What is total productive maintenance? What does it seek to accomplish?

- What gave birth to the concept of continuous improvement? How is it different from innovation? How is it measured?

✦ What are process-improvement tools? How can each of these seven tools be used?

Glossary

Process Management	The control, or planning and administering the activities necessary to sustain high levels of performance in a process, and improvement, or identifying opportunities for achieving continuously higher levels in operational performance.
Control	The planning and administering of activities necessary to sustain high levels of performance in a process.
Improvement	The identifying of opportunities for achieving continuously higher levels in operational performance.
Core Processes	Business processes that most affect customer satisfaction, specifically ones that drive the creation of products and services.
Support Processes	The business processes that are critical to production and delivery.
Quality Control	The business function dedicated to prevent, detect, and correct product or service nonconformances that would make the product or service unfit for use.
Acceptance Sampling	The common practice of accepting or rejecting entire lots of materials procured from suppliers if materials selected for testing do not meet quality control standards.
Attribute	A characteristic that assumes one of two values; for example, present or not present.
Variable	A type of measurement for characteristics on a continuous scale; for example, length or weight.
One-Hundred-Percent Inspection	The inspection of every unit produced.
Sampling Procedures	A procedure in which only a portion of a production lot is inspected.

POKA-YOKE	A device that permanently prevents the recurrence of the defect that it is designed to eliminate.
SUCCESSIVE CHECKING	When processes are designed so they will be physically impossible if preceding processes have produced defective parts.
SELF-CHECKING	A method of quality control similar to successive checking except that the worker performing the operation has to check his or her own output.
AUTONOMATION	The equipping of machines with automatic stopping devices and other features that eliminate the possibility that large quantities of defectives will be produced.
TOTAL PRODUCTIVE MAINTENANCE (TPM)	A maintenance program that is concerned with keeping equipment functionally available so that it will work when needed, perform to expectations in producing a quality product, and perform reliably with no breakdowns.
MEAN TIME BETWEEN FAILURES (MTBF)	The average time between machine failures, calculated by weighting each observation by its probability of occurrence.
KAIZEN	A philosophy of continuous improvement in which it is believed that all improvements in any area of business will enhance the quality of the firm.
DEMING CYCLE	The implementation of the kaizen philosophy in which the cycle broken down into four stages: plan, do, study, and act.
BENCHMARKING	The measuring of performance against the best-in-class companies. It helps a company find its strengths and weaknesses and incorporate practices of industry leaders into its own operations.
REENGINEERING	The rethinking and redesigning of business processes to achieve dramatic improvements in contemporary measures of performance.
ROOT CAUSE	The condition or set of conditions that allowed or caused a defect to occur.
FLOWCHART	A picture of the sequence of steps in a process.
CHECKSHEET	Specialized data-collection forms that facilitate the interpretation of the data.

HISTOGRAM	A descriptive statistic tool that provides a graphical representation of a frequency distribution.
CAUSE-AND-EFFECT DIAGRAM	A graphical tool for organizing a collection of ideas.
PARETO DIAGRAM	A histogram in which frequencies are ordered from largest to smallest.
SCATTER DIAGRAM	The graphical component of a regression analysis used to point out relationships between variables.
RUN CHART	A line graph in which data are plotted over time.
CONTROL CHART	A run chart to which two horizontal lines are added, one called the upper control limit and the other the lower control limit.

SELF-TEST QUESTIONS

MULTIPLE CHOICE

1. Which of the following is **NOT** true of process management?

    A. Is focused on preventing defects and errors.
    B. Attempts to eliminate such waste as non-value-added processing steps.
    C. Has as its goal shorter cycle times.
    D. Has as its goal faster customer responsiveness.
    E. All of the above are true.

2. Any control system must have:

    A. A standard or goal.
    B. A means of measurement of accomplishment.
    C. A means of comparing results with the standard.
    D. Feedback to form the basis for corrective action.
    E. All of the above are true.

3. Which of the following is an objective of quality control?

   A. To determine quality standards for materials and components.
   B. To determine design specifications for the manufacturing process.
   C. To achieve the highest possible quality level for the final product or service.
   D. To answer the complaints from customers.
   E. All of the above are objectives of quality control.

4. The basis for detecting quality problems and identifying areas for improvement is formed by:

   A. Design and predetermined quality standards.
   B. Inspection and measurement.
   C. Conformance and measurement.
   D. Design and inspection.
   E. All of the above.

5. In determining where the inspection site will be:

   A. It is accepted that inspection takes place after each operation.
   B. It is accepted that inspection takes place before each operation.
   C. Site selection is based on economics.
   D. Never inspect until the item is completely finished.

6. The factors that affect manual human inspection are:

   A. Complexity, defect rate, repeated inspections, and inspection rate.
   B. Type of inspection, inspection quantity, and location of inspection activities.
   C. Type of inspection, defect rate, and difficulty of inspection.
   D. Inspection rate and quantity, and the location of inspection activities.

7. Which of the following is **NOT** true of total productive maintenance (TPM)?

   A. TPM involves workers taking responsibility for care and maintenance of their equipment and work space.
   B. TPM focuses on prevention rather than correction.
   C. TPM maximizes overall equipment effectiveness.
   D. TPM schedules downtime to eliminate unplanned downtime.

8. Which of the following is NOT true of Kaizen and innovation:

   A. Kaizen focuses on the long term while innovation focuses on short term.
   B. The principal focus of both is people.
   C. Innovation is dramatic, Kaizen is gradual.
   D. Innovation is usually the result of substantial investment while Kaizen has minimal investment.
   E. Kaizen is process-oriented, innovation is results-oriented.

9. The Deming cycle consists of which four stages?

   A. Study, act, review, and revise.
   B. Evaluate, plan, act, and reevaluate.
   C. Plan, do, study, and act.
   D. Study, plan, act, and revise.

10. Which of the following is NOT true of benchmarking?

    A. Allows the best practices from any industry to be incorporated creatively into a company's operations.
    B. Can only be applied to certain facets of business.
    C. Motivates employees.
    D. Lessens resistance to change.
    E. Broadens peoples' experience base and increases knowledge.

TRUE/FALSE

1. Acceptance sampling is a preferred method of controlling quality.

2. Variable measurement is used when a continuous scale is needed to measure the item being inspected.

3. Statistical process control (SPC) is especially useful after a good quality control system is in place and defect rates are relatively low.

4. The most common quality characteristics in service are time and number of nonconformances.

5. Kaizen is focused on gradual improvements over the long term while innovation focuses on short-term radical changes.

6. Process benchmarking is used for products and services and might be applied to pricing, technical quality, features, and other performance characteristics.

7. A flowchart helps operations managers and the workers involved in process understand the process.

8. Checksheets make it easy to visualize the distribution of amounts, to estimate the average value, or to obtain better information.

9. A Pareto diagram is simply a cause-and-effect diagram in which frequencies are ordered from largest to smallest.

10. In a TQM environment, incoming inspection becomes unnecessary as long-term partnerships are built with suppliers.

FILL IN THE BLANK

1. To apply the techniques of process management, processes must be _____ and _____.

2. Using statistical methods to control quality while a process is operating is called _____ _____ _____.

3. Controlling a process consists of identifying and removing the special causes of _____.

4. _____ costs can contribute significantly to the total cost of sales and have been increasing two to three times as fast as overall production costs.

5. One productivity improvement program, _____ _____, is based on the theory that workers best know their jobs and if trained in simple steps, workers themselves should be the ones to make improvements to the process.

6. _____ goals force an organization to think in a radically different way, to encourage major improvements as well as incremental ones.

7. _____ benchmarking examines how companies compete, seeking the winning strategies that led to competitive advantage and market success.

8. A cause-and-effect diagram is also called an _____ diagram or a _____ diagram.

9. A run chart is a line graph in which data are plotted over _____.

10. Inspection of every single unit produced is called _____ inspection.

CHAPTER 11: PROCESS MANAGEMENT

SELF-TEST PROBLEMS

1. A computer manufacturer has the option of inspecting each chip. If a bad chip is assembled, the cost of disassembly and replacement after the final test and inspection is $2.75. Each chip can be tested for 40 cents. Perform a break-even analysis to determine the percent nonconforming for which 100-percent inspection is better than no inspection.

2. Brendan Aircraft Division operates computerized plotting machines used for aircraft design. The machines are highly reliable, with the exception for 4 ink pens built into the machines that clog constantly. The probability of failure is shown below.

Hours Between Failure	100	110	120	130	140
Probability of Failure	.15	.25	.35	.20	.05

   A failure due to clogged pens results in downtime and lost production at a cost of $132 per failure. Managers are considering a preventive-maintenance program that would be implemented after a set number of hours of operation at a cost of $50. Should the program be implemented and, if so, after how many hours of operation? Assume an 8 hour work day, 5 days a week, 52 weeks a year.

116 PART III: DESIGNING AND MANAGING PRODUCTION PROCESSES

KEY TO SELF-TEST QUESTIONS

MULTIPLE CHOICE

1. E
2. E
3. C
4. B
5. C
6. A
7. D
8. B
9. C
10. B

TRUE/FALSE

1. F
2. T
3. F
4. T
5. T
6. F
7. T
8. T
9. F
10. T

FILL IN THE BLANK

1. repeatable; measurable
2. statistical process control
3. variation
4. Maintenance
5. work simplification
6. Stretch
7. Strategic
8. Ishikawa; fishbone
9. time
10. one-hundred-percent

KEY TO SELF-TEST PROBLEMS

1. C1 = $.40
   C2 = $2.75

   C1/C2 = .145

   If the actual error rate is greater than .145, 100-percent inspection is best.

2. $MTBF = 100(.15) + 110(.25) + 120(.35) + 130(.20) + 140(.05)$
    $= 117.5$

    Current cost with no inspection $= (2080/117.5)(\$132)$
    $= \$2336.68$

TIME BETWEEN INSPECTIONS	NUMBER OF INSPECTIONS PER YEAR	PROBABILITY OF FAILURE BEFORE NEXT INSPECTION	PREVENTIVE MAINTENANCE ($)	FAILURE COST ($)	TOTAL COST ($)
100	20.8	.00	1040.00	0.00	1040.00
110	18.9	.15	945.00	374.22	1319.22
120	17.3	.40	865.00	913.44	1778.44
130	16.0	.75	800.00	1584.00	2384.00
140	14.9	.95	745.00	1868.46	2613.46

To minimize cost, inspection should occur every 100 hours.

Chapter 12
Statistical Quality Control

LEARNING OBJECTIVES

Chapter 12 discusses Statistical Process Control (SPC), a technique that focuses on the process rather than the product and is a prevention-oriented strategy of inspection. The use of control charts for quality control is introduced and methods of constructing control charts for different types of data measurements are shown. Application of these control charts in manufacturing and service organizations is also presented. Finally, acceptance sampling is introduced, a technique used to make a decision about whether to accept or reject a lot based on inspecting a sample. You should concentrate your attention on the following topics:

- What is Statistical Process Control, and what benefits can be gained from using it?

- What are the two types of inspection measurements and how is each different from the other?

- What are the benefits of using control charts?

- List the different types of control charts and describe what each one is used for.

- How does one interpret control charts? What types of patterns indicate whether or not a process is in statistical control?

- What are the key factors in the successful implementation of Statistical Process Control?

120 PART III: DESIGNING AND MANAGING PRODUCTION PROCESSES

◆ What is acceptance sampling and how is it used?

◆ What are the advantages of acceptance sampling?

GLOSSARY

STATISTICAL PROCESS CONTROL (SPC)	A methodology for monitoring quality of conformance and eliminating assignable (special) causes of variation in a process.
CONTROL CHART	A graphical tool for describing when a process is in control or out of control. It provides an aid for determining when to search for assignable causes of variation and take protective action.
PROCESS CAPABILITY	Refers to the total variation due to common causes. It is the ability of the production process to produce products within the desired expectations of customers.
PRODUCER'S RISK	The probability of rejecting a lot of good quality. The probability of a type I error.
CONSUMER'S RISK	The probability of accepting a lot of poor quality. The probability of a type II error.
SAMPLING PLAN	A decision rule that can be used to determine whether to reject the lot on the basis of the number of nonconforming items in a sample of items from the lot.

Chapter 12: Statistical Quality Control

Self-Test Questions

Multiple Choice

1. Which of the following is **NOT** a benefit of using control charts?

    A. Provide simple, effective tools for achieving statistical control.
    B. Distinguishes assignable from common causes of variation thereby minimizing confusion, frustration, and cost of misdirected problem-solving efforts.
    C. Provide a common language for communication between the people on different shifts operating a process.
    D. Predicts performance to specification when a process is in statistical control allowing producer and customer to achieve consistent quality levels at stable costs.
    E. All of the above are benefits of using control charts.

2. Which of the following statements is **NOT** true regarding control charts?

    A. The horizontal axis represents time.
    B. The vertical axis represents the value of the statistic computed for the attribute or variable.
    C. The UCL and LCL are chosen so that there is a high probability that sample values will fall randomly between these limits if the process is not in control.
    D. If the process is in control, 99.7 percent of the sample means lie within 3 standard deviation of the true process mean.
    E. Control charts can distinguish between assignable and common causes of variation.

3. A process may be out of control if:

    A. A point occurs outside the control limits.
    B. A large number of points appear above or below the center line.
    C. There is an increasing or decreasing trend shown by the data points.
    D. A wave or cycle pattern exists.
    E. All of the above indicate a process may be out of control.

4. What factor is not important for successful implementation of SPC?

    A. Layout of the process to be controlled.
    B. Education and training of all employees.
    C. Proper calibration and maintenance of all instruments used for quality measurements.
    D. Addressing of one problem at a time.
    E. Top management commitment.

5. Which of the following is **NOT** a reason why control charts sometimes fail in organizations?

   A. Operators do not trust a new tool.
   B. Old habits of dealing with processes that are out of control are hard to break.
   C. Lack of enough training or practice to fully understand the benefits of control charts.
   D. Lack of a plan for corrective action.
   E. Control charts do not always indicate if the process is out of control.

6. In quality control terminology, the probability of rejecting a lot of good quality is commonly referred to as:

   A. Producer's risk.
   B. Lot sentencing.
   C. Consumer's risk.
   D. Sampling plan.
   E. Acceptance sampling.

7. The statistical process control chart that monitors the process mean is the:

   A. c-chart
   B. Pareto chart
   C. p-chart
   D. r-chart
   E. x-chart

8. Monitoring and controlling the proportion of defects generated by a process is the function of a _____ chart.

   A. c-chart
   B. p-chart
   C. u-chart
   D. x-chart
   E. None of the above

9. Attribute measurement:

   A. Is the measurement of variable that can be measured on a continuous scale.
   B. Is usually more difficult than variable measurement.
   C. Is the measurement of a characteristic that assumes one of two values.
   D. For example, is the measurement of characteristics such as length or weight.
   E. In a statistical sense, is more efficient than variable inspection.

10. Acceptance sampling:
    A. Should be performed on nonhomogeneous lots.
    B. Should include large lot sizes if possible.
    C. Is an appropriate tool for determining the percentage of a lot that do not conform to standards.
    D. Is an appropriate tool for determining the average value of a quality characteristic.
    E. Does not provide an assessment of risk in a decision about whether or not to reject a lot.

TRUE/FALSE

1. Traditionally, process-control decisions have been based on a policy of detection.

2. A process is said to be in statistical control if the output of a production process is subject only to special causes.

3. Statistical Process Control is a method used to monitor quality of conformance and eliminate common causes of variation in a process.

4. The necessity of using large samples to obtain a valid statistical results is a drawback in using attribute data for statistical analysis.

5. A key issue to consider in choosing between c- and u-charts is whether or not the sampling unit is constant.

6. A large number of points below the center line on the range chart indicates a potential improvement in the process.

7. Acceptance sampling is relatively inexpensive and particularly well suited to destructive testing situations.

8. For sampling purposes, a lot should consist of items that are not homogeneous.

9. The probability of accepting a lot of poor quality is called the producer's risk.

10. When a process is in statistical control, the only variations in it are caused by special causes.

FILL IN THE BLANK

1. _____ _____ are graphical tools that indicate when a process is in control or out of control.

2. _____ data is expressed as either conforming or nonconforming and usually requires p-, c-, or u-charts.

3. When the size of the sampling unit is constant, a _____ is used to control the total number of nonconformances per unit.

4. _____ measures the total variation due to common causes.

5. _____ _____ is used to make a decision about whether to accept or reject a group of items on the basis of specified quality characteristics.

6. Acceptance sampling is based on a policy of _____.

7. A _____ error occurs when a false null hypothesis is accepted, while a _____ error occurs when a true null hypothesis is rejected.

8. A _____ is a characteristic that can be measured on a continuous scale.

9. The probability of accepting a lot of poor quality is referred to as _____ risk.

10. _____ procedures involve inspecting only a portion of the inspection lot.

KEY TO SELF-TEST QUESTIONS

MULTIPLE CHOICE

1. E
2. C
3. E
4. A
5. E
6. A
7. E
8. B
9. C
10. B

TRUE/FALSE

1. T
2. F
3. F
4. T
5. T
6. T
7. T
8. F
9. F
10. F

FILL IN THE BLANK

1. Control charts
2. Attribute
3. c-chart
4. Process capability
5. Acceptance sampling
6. detection
7. Type II, Type I
8. variable
9. consumer's
10. Sampling

Chapter 13
Materials and Inventory Management

LEARNING OBJECTIVES

***C**hapter 13* introduces materials and inventory management and is considered one of the most important functions of P/OM. Proper management of materials, from purchasing through final assembly, is essential for effective operation of a production process. The strategic importance of inventory in meeting customer-service and financial objectives is discussed. The nature and characteristics of inventory problems are illustrated. The chapter also examines the traditional role of materials and inventory management and presents some economic models for inventory analysis. Concentrate on the following:

- What is materials management?

- What are the five major types of inventory?

- What is the importance of inventory in production?

- What are the responsibilities and activities of the purchasing department?

- What functions do receiving, packaging, shipping and warehousing perform?

- What are the responsibilities of physical distribution?

- What factors affect transportation decisions?

128 PART IV: MANAGING MATERIALS

- What are the different modes of transportation and their characteristics?
- What are the benefits gained from supplier partnerships?
- How has bar coding and radio frequency communications improved management of materials?
- What are the characteristics used to classify inventory problems?
- What type of costs are associated with inventory?
- How does the ABC inventory analysis system work?
- How is the continuous-review system different from the periodic-review system?
- What assumptions are made when using the EOQ model?
- What is a service level?

GLOSSARY

MATERIALS MANAGEMENT — Management of all of the functions related to the complete cycle of materials flows, including the purchase and internal control of materials, the planning and control of work in process, and the warehousing, shipping, and distribution of end items.

INVENTORY — Any idle goods or materials that are held for future use.

LOT-SIZE INVENTORY — The purchase or production of raw materials and components in large amounts, usually to obtain quantity discounts or truckload-discount transportation rates.

WORK-IN-PROCESS INVENTORIES (WIP) — Inventories used as buffers between work centers or departments in order to enable the production system to continue operating when machines break down, when supplier shipments are late, or when a large proportion of parts is defective.

Chapter 13: Materials and Inventory Management

FLUCTUATION INVENTORY	Also called safety stock. Inventories used to minimize the risk of stockouts. A stockout can result from uncertainties in supply, lead time, and demand.
SAFETY STOCK	The amount of stock added to the normal reorder point to ensure that a desired service level can be maintained.
ANTICIPATION INVENTORY	Inventories built up during the off-season in order to meet future estimated demand.
PURCHASING	Process of acquiring raw materials, component parts, tools, and any other items from outside suppliers.
PROCUREMENT	Another name for purchasing.
BLANKET CONTRACT	An agreement in which a large quantity is contracted for delivery over a long period of time and delivery dates are not specified.
RECEIVING	Involves the unloading of inbound goods from transportation vehicles, verifying that proper quantities are received in good condition and satisfy quality standards, and preparing the goods for storage.
PACKAGING	The department responsible for ensuring that finished goods are correctly labeled and packaged properly to prevent damage.
SHIPPING	The department responsible to for ensuring that finished goods are loaded onto the right transportation vehicle.
WAREHOUSING	Management of materials while they are in storage. A warehouse physically maintains inventory and coordinates receiving and shipping.
PHYSICAL DISTRIBUTION	The department responsible for selecting transportation carriers, managing company-owned fleets of vehicles, and controlling interplant movement of materials and goods.
TRAFFIC	A term used to describe the daily operations of managing the transportation function.

SUPPLIER-CERTIFICATION PROGRAM
A program designed to evaluate suppliers according to various criteria such as quality, cost, and delivery. Florida Power and Light has a three-tiered supplier-certification program to identify "Quality Vendors", "Certified Vendors", and "Excellent Vendors."

BAR CODE
A label consisting of thin black bars separated by spaces that is placed on products. An optical scanner is used to read the information on these labels.

RADIO FREQUENCY (RF) COMMUNICATION
Hardware consisting of either hand-held or truck-mounted units that allow information to be sent to workers electronically from a central computer.

LEAD TIME
The amount of time between the placement of an order and when it is received.

ORDERING COSTS
Costs incurred because of the work involved in placing purchase orders with vendors and organizing the ordered items for production within a plant.

INVENTORY HOLDING COSTS
Also called carrying costs. Includes all expenses incurred as a result of carrying inventory. Examples are cost of capital, breakage, pilferage, obsolescence, etc.

COST OF CAPITAL
The product of the value of a unit of inventory, the length of time held, and the interest rate associated with a dollar tied up in inventory.

GOODWILL COSTS
Lost profit opportunities and possible future loss of revenues resulting from lost sales.

ABC CLASSIFICATION
A management tool for identifying and controlling important inventory items. It is the process of dividing inventory items into three classes on the basis of dollar usage.

INVENTORY POSITION
The amount of inventory on-hand plus any amount on order but not yet received minus back orders.

CONTINUOUS-REVIEW SYSTEM
A type of inventory-control system where the inventory position is continuously monitored. An order for a

Chapter 13: Materials and Inventory Management

predetermined quantity is placed if the inventory position has reached a certain minimum level-reorder point.

Reorder Point — That point in inventory level that defines when the next order should be placed.

Periodic-Review System — A type of inventory-control system where the inventory position is checked only at fixed intervals of time. An order of variable size is placed on the basis of expected needs.

Cycle Counting — A system for continuous physical counting of inventory throughout the year. It allows scheduling of physical counts to ensure that all parts are counted and that higher value parts are counted more frequently than lower value parts.

Economic Order Quantity (EOQ) — Optimal order quantity that minimizes total annual inventory holding costs plus ordering costs, given certain assumptions.

Constant-demand Rate — A condition where the quantity taken form inventory each period of time is constant.

Lead-Time-Demand Distribution — A probability distribution that is created to illustrate possible demand levels during the time that lapses between placing and receiving an order. It is used to determine the reorder point of products that do not have constant demand.

Service Level — The probability that a stockout will not occur during lead time.

132 PART IV: MANAGING MATERIALS

SELF-TEST QUESTIONS

MULTIPLE CHOICE

1. The responsibilities of selecting transportation carriers, managing company-owned fleets of vehicles, and controlling interplant movement of materials and goods belong to:
    A. Purchasing.
    B. Receiving.
    C. Physical distribution.
    D. Packaging and shipping.
    E. Warehousing.

2. A factor that is **NOT** critical in transportation decisions is:
    A. Frequency.
    B. Cost.
    C. Accessibility.
    D. Capability.
    E. Speed.

3. The benefit of supplier partnerships is:
    A. The total number of suppliers can be reduced.
    B. Companies can reduce inventories and incoming inspection and testing.
    C. Suppliers are more willing to invest in process and system improvements.
    D. Suppliers' experts can be brought in at the early stages to take advantage of their specialized knowledge.
    E. All of the above are benefits of supplier partnerships.

4. The phrase "demand derived from the demand for other products" is describing:
    A. Independent demand..
    B. Dependent demand.
    C. Deterministic demand.
    D. Stochastic demand.
    E. Recursive demand.

CHAPTER 13: MATERIALS AND INVENTORY MANAGEMENT

5. Which of the following statements about the EOQ model is **TRUE**?

    A. If annual demand were to double, the EOQ would increase.
    B. If annual demand were to double, both the EOQ and the number of orders per year would increase.
    C. If the carrying cost were to increase, the EOQ would fall.
    D. If the ordering cost were to double, the EOQ would rise.
    E. All of the above statements are true.

6. Inventory that is built up during the off-season to satisfy future estimated demand is called:

    A. Fluctuation inventory.
    B. Anticipation inventory.
    C. Lot-size inventory.
    D. Work-in-process inventory.
    E. Seasonal inventory.

7. Which of the following is **NOT** a responsibility of the purchasing department?

    A. Learning the material needs of the organization.
    B. Selecting qualified suppliers.
    C. Purchasing transportation services.
    D. Monitoring cost, quality, and delivery performance.
    E. Negotiating price.

8. Costs associated with lost sales are an example of:

    A. Ordering costs.
    B. Holding costs.
    C. Carrying costs.
    D. Goodwill costs.
    E. Cost of capital.

9. When measuring inventory-management performance, inventory can be classified into each of the following categories **EXCEPT**:

    A. Operating inventory.
    B. Anticipation inventory.
    C. Excess inventory.
    D. Obsolete inventory.
    E. Surplus inventory.

10. Inventory problems are classified by:

    A. Number of items.
    B. The nature of demand.
    C. Lead time and stockouts.
    D. The number of time periods in planning horizon.
    E. All of the above.

TRUE/FALSE

1. High levels of work-in-process inventories can limit a firm's flexibility and can hide problems such as unreliable machines, late supplier shipments, or defective parts.

2. ABC analysis is based on the presumption that all items must be tightly controlled to produce important cost savings.

3. A two-bin system is an example of a periodic-review inventory control system.

4. The EOQ model minimizes the total cost by balancing the inventory holding cost and the ordering cost.

5. In inventory management, ordering costs become relevant to inventory decisions only when a quantity discount is available.

6. The cost of capital invested in inventory normally accounts for the largest component of inventory-holding costs.

7. The most accessible mode of transportation is motor carriers.

8. In ABC inventory analysis "A" items account for a small dollar value but a large percentage of total items.

9. The EOQ model is concerned with the decisions of how much to order and when to place an order.

10. Lead time is the amount of time between the placement of an order and when it is shipped.

FILL IN THE BLANK

1. _____ is any idle goods or materials that are held for future use.

2. _____ is a mode of transportation that has limited use and accessibility and is used primarily for such products as oil and natural gas.

3. The type of inventory control system where the inventory position is checked only at fixed intervals of time is called _____-_____ system.

4. _____ _____ is the probability that a stockout will not occur during lead time.

5. _____ costs are incurred each time a company places an order with a supplier or a production order with its own shop.

6. _____ _____ is a system for continuous physical counting of inventory throughout the year.

7. The purchase or production of raw materials and components in large amounts, usually to obtain quantity discounts or truckload-discount transportation rates, is called _____-_____ inventory.

8. An agreement in which a large quantity is contracted for delivery over a long period of time and delivery dates are not specified is referred to as a _____ _____.

9. _____ _____ is the point in inventory level that defines when the next order should be placed.

10. A label consisting of thin black bars separated by spaces that is placed on products is called _____ _____.

136 PART IV: MANAGING MATERIALS

SELF-TEST PROBLEMS

1. A firm stocks a certain item for which inventory management is continuous review. The annual demand for the item is 20,000 units. Ordering costs are $25 per order and inventory holding cost is $4 per unit per year. The firm operates for 365 days each year and the lead time is 2 days. If the assumptions of EOQ model are applicable, determine:

   A. The EOQ for this item.

   B. The total annual cost.

   C. The cycle time.

   D. The reorder point.

2. Each year the Eagle Corporation purchases 35,000 units of an item that costs $16 per unit. The cost of placing an order is $24, and the holding cost is 25 percent of the unit cost per year. The company is open 5 days a week for 52 weeks per year. The order lead time is 3 days.

   A. Determine the EOQ?

   B. What is the reorder point if a constant demand rate is assumed?

   C. Further investigation revealed that the lead-time demand follows a normal distribution, with a mean of 400 and a standard deviation of 3.65. If a service level of 95 percent is required by Eagle Corp., what is the new reorder point?

   D. Determine the safety stock.

KEY TO SELF-TEST QUESTIONS

MULTIPLE CHOICE

1. C
2. A
3. E
4. B
5. E
6. B
7. C
8. D
9. B
10. E

TRUE/FALSE

1. T
2. F
3. F
4. T
5. F
6. T
7. T
8. F
9. T
10. F

FILL IN THE BLANK

1. Inventory
2. Pipeline
3. periodic-review
4. Service level
5. Ordering
6. Cycle counting
7. lot-size
8. blanket contract
9. Reorder point
10. bar code

KEY TO SELF-TEST PROBLEMS

1. A. The Economic Order Quantity is:

$$Q^* = \sqrt{\frac{2DCo}{Ch}} = \sqrt{\frac{2(20,000)(25)}{4}} = 500 \ units$$

B. Total Annual Cost is:

$$TC = \frac{Q}{2}(Ch) + \frac{D}{Q}(Co)$$
$$= \frac{500}{2}(4) + \frac{20{,}000}{500}(25)$$
$$= 1000 + 1000$$
$$= \$2{,}000$$

C. Cycle Time:

$$T = \frac{Q^*}{D}(365) = \frac{500}{20{,}000}(365) = 9.125 \; days$$

D. Reorder Point is:

$$R = dm$$
$$= \frac{20{,}000}{365}(2)$$
$$= 109.6$$

2. A. The Economic Order Quantity is:

$$Q^* = \sqrt{\frac{2DCo}{Ch}} = \sqrt{\frac{2(35{,}000)(24)}{4}} = 648 \; units$$

B. The Reorder Point is:

$$R = dm$$
$$= \frac{35{,}000}{260}(3)$$
$$= 403.85$$

C. For a 95% Service Level, area in tail = 0.05, Z = 1.645

$$R = \mu + z\sigma$$
$$= 400 + 1.645(3.65)$$
$$= 406$$

D. Safety Stock = 406 - 400 = 6 units

Chapter 14
Decision Models for Inventory Management

LEARNING OBJECTIVES

*C*hapter 14 presents models and approaches for inventory analysis. While quantitative analysis does not necessarily give operations managers the best decision, the models described in this chapter have helped businesses to improve their decision making. Topics that you should focus on include:

- When is it desirable to allow planned shortages in your inventory model? How does this model work?

- How is the production lot-size model similar to the EOQ model? How is it different?

- What is a quantity discount model and why would a company use this model for their inventory system?

- What type of inventory model would a company use if their demand is not constant over time? Can you compare and contrast these inventory models?

- What is the single-period inventory model?

- Why might simulation be applied to inventory analysis? How might it be used?

GLOSSARY

PRODUCTION LOT-SIZE MODEL An inventory-decision model where it is assumed that units are supplied to inventory at a constant rate over several days or weeks.

QUANTITY DISCOUNT Lower unit cost offered by suppliers as an inventory incentive for large purchase quantities.

PERIODIC-ORDER-QUANTITY METHOD A method by which the economic order quantity is divided by average demand to yield an economic time interval between orders. Orders are then placed at these intervals for all known future demands.

PART-PERIOD-BALANCING METHOD A method of lot-sizing for dynamic demand that attempts to balance the total costs of ordering and holding.

SILVER-MEAL METHOD A method similar to part-period-balancing in that you consider ordering one period's demand, then two period's demand, and so on, but you stop when average cost per period exceeds that of the previous period.

WAGNER-WHITIN ALGORITHM A method of lot-sizing that provides the true minimum cost. This method implicitly evaluates all possible ways of ordering to meet demand at minimum total cost.

SINGLE-PERIOD INVENTORY MODEL A model that applies to inventory situations in which one order is placed for the product. At the end of the period the product is either sold out or the surplus is sold for salvage value.

SELF-TEST QUESTIONS

MULTIPLE CHOICE

1. It may be desirable to allow for planned shortages in your inventory model when:

    A. Value per unit of inventory is low.
    B. Inventory-holding cost is low.
    C. Value per unit of inventory is very high.
    D. You should never allow shortages in inventory.

2. Which of the following is **NOT** true when comparing the production lot-size model to EOQ:

   A. Both attempt to determine how much we should order of a product.
   B. Only EOQ assumes a constant rate of demand.
   C. The models determine when the order should be placed.
   D. The models differ on whether goods arrive in one shipment or over a period of time.
   E. All of the above are true.

3. The ordering cost in a production lot-size model is called production-setup cost because:

   A. It includes labor hours, material, and lost production time.
   B. It is a fixed cost for every production run.
   C. Its cost varies with the quantity produced.
   D. Its costs are incurred after production has began.
   E. All of the above are true.

4. Of the following models, the one that is **NOT** used for dynamic demand is:

   A. Periodic-order-quantity.
   B. Part-period balancing.
   C. Silver-meal.
   D. Single-period inventory.
   E. All of the above are appropriate for dynamic demand.

5. For dynamic demand, the inventory method that calculates the economic time interval between orders is:

   A. Silver-Meal.
   B. Part-period balancing.
   C. Wagner-Whitin.
   D. Periodic-order-quantity.

6. In order to simulate an inventory system, your system must have:

   A. Constant demand.
   B. Dynamic demand.
   C. Shortages allowed.
   D. No quantity discounts allowed.
   E. Any system can be simulated.

TRUE/FALSE

1. In planned shortage inventory models, negative inventory represents the number of back orders.

2. A constant supply rate implies that your supplier has formally agreed to supply you with goods as needed, so that you will have a constant, reliable source.

3. Quantity discounts are lower unit costs offered by suppliers as an incentive for large purchase quantities.

4. The goal of lot-sizing for dynamic demand is to determine a schedule that will minimize total cost.

5. If there is surplus inventory remaining in a single-period inventory model, the order quantity is adjusted before the next order is placed.

6. Simulation is an important decision making tool because it has the flexibility to model unique features of the system that are difficult to represent in pure mathematic terms.

FILL IN THE BLANK

1. _____ _____ is the cost, or loss, that is incurred when customers must wait for their orders.

2. In the production lot-size model, the size of the production run is called _____ _____.

3. Ordering cost in the production lot-size model is more correctly called _____ cost.

4. A fundamental assumption behind the EOQ model is that demand is _____ over time.

5. The lot-sizing method for dynamic demand that gives the true minimum total cost is the _____ _____.

6. If inventory items are seasonal or perishable, the most appropriate inventory model would be the _____ _____ model.

CHAPTER 14: DECISION MODELS FOR INVENTORY MANAGEMENT 145

SELF-TEST PROBLEMS

1. Greenleaf Nursery sells Super Grow fertilizer. The annual demand for this fertilizer is 11,0000 bags. The fertilizer costs $8.75 per bag, and the nursery's holding-cost rate is 20 percent. The cost of ordering from the supplier is $105. The owner would like to maintain a high level of customer satisfaction, but is considering allowing backorders to reduce costs. The owner estimates that back-order cost would be $150 per year. What should he do?

2. Happy Farms Dairy makes cheese to supply stores in their region. Demand is fairly steady at 5000 pounds per month. They are equipped to produce as much as 7000 pounds per month after they have set up the production process. The cost of setting up the production line is $250, the production cost is $1.35 per pound of cheese. Happy Farms has a 3-percent monthly inventory-holding cost. What production lot size would you recommend?

146 PART IV: MANAGING MATERIALS

3. Handy Man Hardware Wholesalers, Inc., orders power mowers from a major mid-western manufacturer. The following quantity discount schedule applies to 21 inch self-propelled, electric start, rotary power mowers:

ORDER SIZE	DISCOUNT (%)	UNIT COST ($)
0 to 199	0	90.00
200 to 499	5	85.50
500 or more	8	82.80

Annual demand is 1000 units, ordering cost is $10 per order, and annual inventory-holding cost is 10 percent. What should the order quantity be?

KEY TO SELF-TEST QUESTIONS

MULTIPLE CHOICE

1. C
2. B
3. A
4. D
5. D
6. E

TRUE/FALSE

1. T
2. F
3. T
4. T
5. F
6. T

FILL IN THE BLANK

1. Goodwill cost
2. lot quantity or production lot size
3. production-setup
4. constant
5. Wagner-Whitin algorithm
6. single-period inventory

KEY TO SELF-TEST PROBLEMS

1. The EOQ without backorders:

$$Q^* = \sqrt{\frac{2(11000)(105)}{.2(8.75)}} = 1148.9 = 1149$$

The total annual inventory cost using an EOQ of 1149 is:

$$TC = \frac{1}{2}(1149)(.2)(8.75) + \frac{11,000}{1149}(105) = \$2,010.60$$

The optimal order-quantity and backorder levels are:

$$Q* = \sqrt{\frac{2(11{,}000)\,(105)}{(.2)\,(8.75)} * \frac{1.75 + 150}{150}} = 1155.6 = 1156$$

$$S* = 1156 * \frac{1.75}{1.75 + 150} = 13.33 = 14$$

$$TC = \frac{(1156 - 14)^2}{2(1156)} * .2(8.75) + \frac{11{,}000}{1156} * 105 + \frac{14^2}{2(1156)} * 150 = \$1{,}999.00$$

Do permit backorders.

2.
$$Q* = \sqrt{\frac{2(5000)\,(250)}{1 - \frac{5000}{7000} * (.03)\,(1.35)}}$$

$$= 14{,}699.5 = 14{,}700$$

3.
$$Q1 = \sqrt{\frac{2(1000)(10)}{.1(90)}} = 47.1 = 48$$

$$Q2 = \sqrt{\frac{2(1000)(10)}{.1(85.50)}} = 48.4 = 49; \text{ using } Q \text{ of } 200$$

$$Q3 = \sqrt{\frac{2(1000)(10)}{.1(82.30)}} = 49.3 = 50; \text{ using } Q \text{ of } 500$$

$$TC1 = \frac{10(1000)}{48} + .1(90)(\frac{48}{2}) + 1000(90) = \$90{,}424.33$$

$$TC2 = \frac{10(1000)}{200} + .1(85.5)(\frac{200}{2}) + 1000(85.5) = \$86{,}405.00$$

$$TC3 = \frac{10(1000)}{500} + .1(82.5)(\frac{500}{2}) + 1000(82.8) = \$84{,}882.50$$

Order in lots of 500.

Chapter 15
Lean Production and Synchronous Manufacturing

LEARNING OBJECTIVES

*C**hapter 15* introduces lean production and synchronous manufacturing and addresses how these concepts have changed the nature of manufacturing. The chapter discusses in detail the philosophy of JIT, which is one approach to synchronous manufacturing, as well as what changes are necessary to make JIT work effectively. You should focus on the following:

- How did the "Toyota production system" change the nature of manufacturing worldwide?

- What is JIT? What are the six categories by which the core elements of JIT are classified? How do these categories relate to JIT and to each other?

- How does JIT link to management practices?

- What are the benefits of JIT production?

- What are some applications of JIT in service organizations?

- What is constraint management? What is its principle objective?

Glossary

Lean Production — The elimination of waste, reduction of inventories, improvement of quality, and the development of human resources.

Synchronous Manufacturing — Any systematic method of moving material quickly and smoothly through the productive resources of a manufacturing facility in response to market demand.

Just-In-Time (JIT) — An approach to synchronous manufacturing in which the objective is to eliminate all sources of waste, including unnecessary inventory and scrap.

Constraint Management — An approach to synchronous manufacturing which is based on the idea of effectively exploiting a company's limited resources.

Pull Production — A system in which items are delivered or produced only when they are required. It begins at final assembly and works backward through all workstations in the production process.

Kanban — An information system in which the type and number of units required by a process are written on Kanbans, or cards, and used to initiate withdrawal and production of items through the production process.

Level Master Schedule — A schedule by which small lot sizes of each product are made every day and even every hour.

Bakayake — A method to ensure that no defective parts are allowed to flow in the system. It involves the use of automatic devices to stop machines if quality deteriorates.

Theory of Constraints (TOC) — An approach to synchronous manufacturing whose objective is to establish a process of continuous improvement. It is based on the premise that constraints determine the performance of any system.

CHAPTER 15: LEAN PRODUCTION AND SYNCHRONOUS MANUFACTURING

SELF-TEST QUESTIONS

MULTIPLE CHOICE

1. Which of the following is **NOT** true of the JIT philosophy today?

    A. It is aimed at eliminating all forms of waste.
    B. Tries to improve quality.
    C. Addresses productivity.
    D. Examines what adds value to the product.
    E. All of the above are true.

2. Short setup times:

    A. Work best for long production runs.
    B. Enable the manufacturer to make frequent changeovers.
    C. Provide manufacturers with less flexibility.
    D. Do not help with a company's strategic objectives.
    E. All of the above are true.

3. To operate smoothly, a JIT system must:

    A. Make finished-product lot sizes large.
    B. Produce according to demand.
    C. Minimize fluctuations in production demand.
    D. Have a level master schedule for varying lot sizes.

4. JIT production requires:

    A. A smooth flow in which materials introduced at one end of the process move without delay to finished product.
    B. A layout that may be in a straight line.
    C. A layout that may be U-shaped cells.
    D. The use of group technology.
    E. All of the above are true.

5. The three key JIT practices based on yo-l-don management-employee relationship are:

    A. Multifunction workers, small-group problem solving, and training.
    B. Education, empowering employees, and human resources.
    C. Quality circles, limited responsibility, and maximized flexibility.
    D. Subdivision of labor, increased job efficiency, and more responsibility.

6. In which of the following areas does JIT purchasing **NOT** differ from conventional purchasing:

   A. Delivery lot sizes.
   B. Timing of deliveries.
   C. Amount of inventory.
   D. Length of purchasing agreements.
   E. All of the above are true.

7. Suppliers are rewarded with long-term contracts in return for accommodating JIT manufacturers with:

   A. Fewer deliveries, standardized shipments, and better quality.
   B. More frequent deliveries, standardized shipments, and better quality.
   C. More frequent deliveries, nonstandardized shipments, and better quality.
   D. Fewer deliveries, nonstandardized shipments, and better quality.

8. A major problem for managers who are trying to implement JIT is:

   A. Increased worker involvement and empowerment.
   B. Securing worker cooperation.
   C. Training.
   D. Maintaining new job classifications.
   E. Development programs.

9. Which of the following is **NOT** is benefit of JIT production:

   A. Cost.
   B. Improved quality.
   C. Lower expenditures for facilities, equipment, and labor.
   D. Use of more sophisticated inventory-control systems.
   E. All of the above are true.

10. The fundamental purpose of JIT is:

    A. Elimination of waste.
    B. Lengthening of cycle time.
    C. Continuous improvement.
    D. Better facilities and equipment.
    E. All of the above are true.
    F. A and C are both true.

Chapter 15: Lean Production and Synchronous Manufacturing

True/False

1. The concept of lean production was developed at Toyota Motor Company.

2. Ordering costs can be reduced with small lot sizes as small lots can be delivered directly to production, eliminating costly receiving activities.

3. In JIT, excess work-in-process easily compensates for equipment breakdowns.

4. Kanbans are used to initiate withdrawal and production of items through the production process.

5. Poor equipment layout is one of the major causes of inefficiency in manufacturing.

6. The role of purchasing in JIT is no different from conventional practice.

7. JIT overcomes the importance of geographic proximity for purchasing.

8. Some traditional cost-accounting practices contribute to the kind of waste that JIT systems are designed to eliminate.

9. JIT production requires many internal and external changes for an organization.

10. The Japanese train special groups of workers to serve as quality inspectors.

Fill in the Blanks

1. A continuous flow of _____ lot sizes minimizes unnecessary inventory investment.

2. Most factories use a system of _____ production in which they make parts and then send them to subsequent operations or to storage.

3. _____ manufacturing keeps inventories and lead times lower than batch or job-shop production, thus leading to increased productivity and lower cost.

4. The idea that employees be empowered to make important decisions such as stopping production when a problem is identified is called _____.

5. _____ problem solving encourages workers to bring production-related problems and ideas for improvement to team problem-solving sessions.

6. JIT purchasing requires that the manufacturer trust the supplier to deliver on time and with _____ defects.

7. The Japanese use a method called _____ to ensure that no defective parts are allowed to flow in the system.

8. The most obvious benefit from using JIT is the cost benefit resulting from a reduction in _____ inventory.

9. A _____ is any resource lack that prevents the system from achieving continuously higher levels of performance.

10. TOC assumes that material flows in small batches called _____ _____ that consist of the required number of units that need to be processed before the next operation is done.

Chapter 15: Lean Production and Synchronous Manufacturing

Key to Self-Test Questions

Multiple Choice

1. E
2. B
3. C
4. E
5. A
6. E
7. B
8. A
9. D
10. F

True/False

1. T
2. T
3. F
4. T
5. T
6. F
7. F
8. T
9. T
10. F

Fill in the Blanks

1. small
2. push
3. Repetitive
4. yo-i-don
5. Small-group
6. zero
7. bakayake
8. WIP
9. constraint
10. transfer batches

Chapter 16
Aggregate Production Planning and Master Scheduling

LEARNING OBJECTIVES

*C*hapter 16 introduces aggregate-production planning and master scheduling. These tools are used to determine the future production levels over a time horizon of several months to one year. The production plan establishes an intermediate-range goal for the company's products and capacity utilization in total. The master schedule provides the input for detailed scheduling and control at the operational level. Key planning strategies for meeting fluctuating demand are discussed. Several quantitative approaches to developing low-cost production plans are described. Capacity planning strategies for service organizations are also discussed. Concentrate on the following:

- What are the essential elements of the production-planning and scheduling process?

- How is aggregate-production planning different from master production scheduling?

- What is the first step in production planning process?

- What are the strategies used for dealing with fluctuating demand?

- What are the disadvantages of the work-force changes strategy?

- How is inventory smoothing achieved?

- What are the major costs associated with implementing a production plan?

158 PART V: PLANNING AND SCHEDULING

- ✦ How is the level production strategy different from the chase-demand strategy?

- ✦ What are the various quantitative approaches to aggregate production planning?

- ✦ What is the importance of a master production schedule?

- ✦ What is uniform plant loading and what is its purpose?

- ✦ How does capacity planning in service organizations differ from capacity planning in manufacturing organizations.

- ✦ What are the two main strategies used in short-term capacity planning for service organizations? Give some examples of each.

GLOSSARY

AGGREGATE PRODUCTION PLANNING	The development of monthly or quarterly production requirements for product groups or families that will meet the estimates of demand.
MASTER PRODUCTION SCHEDULE (MPS)	Time-phased production requirements for individual products extracted from the aggregate production plan.
ROUGH-CUT CAPACITY PLANNING	The analysis of the master production schedule (MPS) to determine if sufficient capacity exists at critical points (bottlenecks) in the production process.
FINAL ASSEMBLY SCHEDULE (FAS)	A statement of the final products that are to be assembled from the master production schedule (MPS).
LEVEL-DEMAND STRATEGY	A production strategy that maintains a level production rate or staff level over the planning horizon.
CHASE-DEMAND STRATEGY	A production strategy that adjusts production rates or staff levels to exactly match forecasted demand requirements over the planning horizon.

CHAPTER 16: AGGREGATE PRODUCTION PLANNING & MASTER SCHEDULING 159

UNIFORM PLANT LOADING (UPL)   A technique used to smooth the variability of demand on a firm's resources.

SELF-TEST QUESTIONS

MULTIPLE CHOICE

1. Poor production planning can lead to:

    A. Excessive inventory levels.
    B. Increased carrying costs.
    C. Increased back orders.
    D. Reduced customer service.
    E. All of the above.

2. The aggregate-planning strategy where inventory is built up during slack periods to satisfy demand during peak periods is called:

    A. Production-rate changes.
    B. Work-force changes.
    C. Inventory smoothing.
    D. Demand shifting.
    E. Inventory-level changes.

3. An example of an industry where the aggregate planning strategy of work-force changes would **NOT** be cost-effective is:

    A. High-tech industry.
    B. Agriculture industry.
    C. Toy industry.
    D. Tourist industry.
    E. None of the above.

4. Which of the following is **NOT** a major cost associated with implementing a production plan?

   A. Costs of production.
   B. Inventory ordering costs.
   C. Inventory holding costs.
   D. Stockout costs.
   E. Capacity change costs.

5. _____ will find a minimum-cost production plan when variable sources of production are available, when production and inventory costs are linear and when there is a limited capacity for each production source in each time period.

   A. Heuristic approach.
   B. Transportation model.
   C. Linear programming.
   D. Trial and error method.
   E. Scoring model.

6. Uniform plant loading:

   A. Smooths the variability of demand on a firm's resources.
   B. Is a key component of just-in-time production.
   C. Attempts to produce the same quantity of each end item each day.
   D. Minimizes expediting, rework, and other delays and makes disruptions less likely.
   E. All of the above.

7. Which of the following is **NOT** a method of controlling supply in service organizations?

   A. Use of part-time or seasonal employees.
   B. Shifting of work to slack periods.
   C. Cross training employees to perform different tasks thus creating flexibility.
   D. Development of new service packages to utilize idle capacity during off-peak times.
   E. Increasing customer participation in the service process.

8. All of the following are characteristics of work-force changes strategy **EXCEPT**:

   A. Low employee morale.
   B. High training costs.
   C. Seniority bumping which alters the skills of the work force.
   D. Planned overtime and subcontracting during periods of peak demand.
   E. Severance pay and additional unemployment insurance costs.

CHAPTER 16: AGGREGATE PRODUCTION PLANNING & MASTER SCHEDULING   161

9. A survey of industry practice in production planning showed that when companies assess the various production-planning strategies, less importance is placed on:

    A. Overtime costs.
    B. Layoff costs.
    C. Shortage costs.
    D. Hiring costs.
    E. Holding costs.

10. A rapid determination of the feasibility of a production schedule is provided by:

    A. Aggregate production planning.
    B. Final assembly schedule.
    C. Rough-cut capacity planning.
    D. Uniform plant loading.
    E. Production schedule.

TRUE/FALSE

1. The master schedule establishes an intermediate-range goal for the company's products and capacity utilization in total.

2. Seniority bumping practices can change the skills mix of the work force which results in greater efficiency in production.

3. The inventory smoothing strategy works best for perishable commodities.

4. Capacity planning using overall factors is a rough-cut capacity planning technique which allocates capacity requirements to individual department or work centers on the basis of historical data on work loads.

5. Strategies for short-term capacity planning can be grouped into two categories: controlling supply and altering demand.

6. Making products whose seasonal peaks are opposite is an example of smoothing inventory strategy.

7. A chase demand strategy avoids rate changes but can result in excessive inventories and possibly lost sales.

8. The master production schedule is a statement of the final products that are to be assembled from the FAS items.

162 PART V: PLANNING AND SCHEDULING

9. In industries involving assembly operations with low skill requirements, changing work force levels is not a viable alternative.

10. In a make-to-stock industry a net demand forecast is used in formulating the MPS.

FILL IN THE BLANK

1. The development of monthly or quarterly production requirements for product groups or families that will meet the estimates of demand is called _____ _____ _____.

2. _____ _____ is a production strategy that adjusts production rates or staff levels to exactly match forecasted demand requirements over the planning horizon.

3. _____ _____ is a technique used for finding the minimum-cost solution for production-planning problems.

4. For _____-to-_____ industries, known customer orders determine the MPS.

5. Service capacity planning is _____ term.

6. An airline that shares airport gates and baggage handling equipment with another airline is involved in _____ sharing.

7. _____ _____ strategy involves using various marketing strategies to shift some of the demand from peak periods to slack periods.

8. Telephone rates are reduced during evenings and weekends to stimulate demand during off peak hours is a method of altering demand through _____ _____ schemes.

9. A techniques which smooths the variability of demand on a firm's resources is called _____ _____ _____.

10. Production rates can be altered by using planned _____ and _____.

SELF-TEST PROBLEMS

1. A company that manufactures computer printers has a six week demand forecast for its product as shown in the table below:

WEEK	1	2	3	4	5	6
DEMAND FORECAST	250	460	380	420	550	490

   A. Calculate the cumulative demand for each month and the average demand per week.

   B. Compute the net ending inventory levels for the six week period. Assume a beginning inventory of zero for *week 1* and that all shortages are backordered.

2. The aggregate demand pattern for a particular product is given in the table below. If the unit production cost is $1.10, overtime cost is $1.40, and shortage cost is $1.50, compute the cost of a level production strategy and a chase-demand strategy.

Month	1	2	3	4	5	6	7	8	9	10	11	12
Demand	50	41	58	35	40	75	70	55	62	48	60	56

The inventory holding cost is $0.40 per unit per month. The beginning inventory for both strategies is 3,000. In the case of the level production strategy, assume a desired ending inventory of 7,000. The capacity for regular production is 5,500, and there is an overtime capacity of 1,000 units.

CHAPTER 16: AGGREGATE PRODUCTION PLANNING & MASTER SCHEDULING

KEY TO SELF-TEST QUESTIONS

MULTIPLE CHOICE

1. E
2. C
3. A
4. B
5. B
6. E
7. D
8. D
9. B
10. C

TRUE/FALSE

1. F
2. F
3. F
4. T
5. T
6. T
7. F
8. F
9. F
10. T

FILL IN THE BLANK

1. aggregate production planning
2. Chase demand
3. Linear programming
4. make-to-order
5. short
6. capacity
7. Demand shifting
8. differential pricing
9. uniform plant loading
10. overtime, subcontracting

KEY TO SELF-TEST PROBLEMS

1. A. First, we calculate the cumulative demand:

WEEK	DEMAND	CUMULATIVE
1	250	250
2	460	710
3	380	1090
4	420	1510
5	550	2060
6	490	2550

Now, the average demand is:

$$\frac{2550}{6} = 425 \ printers$$

B. Net ending inventory is shown below:

WEEK	DEMAND	PRODUCTION	CUMULATIVE	NET ENDING
1	250	425	425	175
2	460	425	850	140
3	380	425	1275	185
4	420	425	1700	190
5	550	425	2125	65
6	490	425	2550	0

2. A. For the level-production strategy:

Beginning inventory is 3,000, ending inventory is 7,000, total demand is 65,000

$$Average \ production \ level = \frac{65,000 - 3,000 + 7,000}{12} = 5,750$$

CHAPTER 16: AGGREGATE PRODUCTION PLANNING & MASTER SCHEDULING

Using the average production level, we calculate the total cost for each month as shown below:

Month	Demand	Prod.	Inv.	Prod. Cost	Inv. Costs	OT Costs	Short. Costs	Total Costs
1	5000	5750	750	6325	300			6625
2	4100	5750	2400	6325	960			7285
3	5800	5750	2350	6325	940			7265
4	3500	5750	4600	6325	1840			8165
5	4000	5750	6350	6325	2540			8865
6	7500	5750	4600	6325	1840			8165
7	7000	5750	3350	6325	1340			7665
8	6800	5750	2300	6325	920			7245
9	6200	5750	1850	6325	740			7065
10	4800	5750	2800	6325	1120			7445
11	7000	5750	1550	6325	620			6945
12	5600	5750	1700	6325	680			7005

Therefore, the total cost for the level production strategy is $89,740

B. For the chase-demand strategy:
Production is set equal to demand for each month.

The total costs for each month are shown below:

Month	Prod. & Demand	Prod. Costs	Inv. Costs	OT Costs	Short. Costs	Total Costs
1	5000	5500	1200			6700
2	4100	4510	1200			5710
3	5800	6050	1080			7130
4	3500	3850	1080			4930
5	4000	4400	1080			5480
6	7500	6050	280			6330
7	7000	6050	0	1120		7170
8	6800	6050	0	1400	450	7900
9	6200	6050	0	980		7030
10	4800	5280	0			5280
11	7000	6050	0	1400	750	8200
12	5600	6050	0	140		6190

Therefore, the total cost for the chase-demand strategy is $78,050. This is less than the level production strategy total cost.

Chapter 17
Material Requirements Planning

LEARNING OBJECTIVES

*C**hapter 17* describes the use of material requirements planning (MRP) as a tool for planning and controlling manufacturing inventories. This method determines the requirements and schedules for dependent demand items such as raw materials, components, and subassemblies. The chapter discusses the planning and implementation of MRP. The benefits as well as reasons for failure of the MRP system are presented. Manufacturing resource planning is introduced and several contrasting production-planning philosophies are discussed. Concentrate on the following:

- What is the purpose of MRP?

- What type of inventory is controlled by MRP systems?

- What are the key inputs to the MRP system?

- What are the three major functions of an MRP system?

- What is the function of the bill of materials in an MRP system?

- What is contained in an inventory record?

- What does the term time phasing mean?

- How are net-component requirements calculated?

- How is the regeneration approach of updating net requirements different from the net-change approach.

- What is capacity requirements planning and how is it calculated?

- What is a closed-loop MRP system?

- What are the major causes of MRP failures?

- How can MRP be applied in service organizations?

- What is the difference between MRP and MRP II?

- What are the principal attributes of MRP II?

- How is JIT different from MRP?

Glossary

Material Requirements Planning (MRP)	A technique used to plan for and control manufacturing inventories.
Bucket	Principal unit of time measurement in a material requirements planning system; usually one week in length.
Time Phasing	The process of "backing up" from the time the component or assembly is required by the amount of that item's lead time to show when the production of each component or assembly must be carried out in order to complete the final product by a specified date.
Regeneration Approach	An approach for updating net requirements where the entire materials plan is recalculated periodically.

NET-CHANGE APPROACH	Another approach for updating net requirements where the MRP system recalculates requirements whenever necessary but only for those components affected by the change.
CAPACITY REQUIREMENTS PLANNING (CRP)	The process of determining labor and machine resources required to accomplish the tasks of production.
MANUFACTURING RESOURCE PLANNING (MRPII)	The process of planning all resources of a firm, including business planning, production planning, master production scheduling, material requirements planning, and capacity requirements planning.

SELF-TEST QUESTIONS

MULTIPLE CHOICE

1. Material requirements planning (MRP) is used to plan for and control:

    A. Independent demand inventories.
    B. Dependent demand inventories.
    C. Safety stocks.
    D. Anticipation inventories.
    E. None of the above.

2. Which of the following is **NOT** a major function of an MRP system?

    A. Control of inventory levels.
    B. Assignment of priorities for components.
    C. Detailed capacity planning.
    D. Rough cut capacity planning.
    E. All of the above are major functions.

3. An item that does **NOT** exhibit dependent demand characteristics is:

   A. Cars.
   B. Raw materials.
   C. Components.
   D. Subassemblies.
   E. Work in process.

4. In an MRP system, the file containing the BOM is called:

   A. Load file.
   B. Item record file.
   C. Product structure file.
   D. Component file.
   E. Inventory file.

5. Typical information contained in an inventory record is:

   A. Part number of the item
   B. On-hand quantity
   C. On-order quantity
   D. Procurement lead time
   E. All of the above

6. The quantity of the component needed to support production at the next higher level of assembly is referred to as:

   A. Gross requirements.
   B. Scheduled receipts.
   C. Planned order releases.
   D. Net requirements.
   E. None of the above.

7. The process of determining the amount of labor and machine resources required to accomplish the tasks of production is called:

   A. Material requirements planning.
   B. Manufacturing resource planning.
   C. Capacity requirements planning.
   D. Resource requirements planning.
   E. Production planning.

8. Inaccurate inventory records are caused by:

   A. Lack of formal receiving procedures.
   B. Unlocked storerooms.
   C. Inappropriate forms or ineffective materials-information systems.
   D. Lack of audit procedures.
   E. All of the above.

9. Which of the following is **NOT** true regarding JIT?

   A. Specialized labor skills are required.
   B. It is well suited for repetitive manufacturing activities.
   C. Production scheduling is demand driven - a pull system.
   D. Few suppliers used and they are treated as part of a team.
   E. Seeks to eliminate all sources of waste in production activities.

10. MRP system failure is usually a result of:

    A. Lack of accuracy.
    B. Lack of realism in data and information.
    C. Inadequate planning.
    D. Inadequate implementation.
    E. All of the above.

TRUE/FALSE

1. The purpose of MRP is to ensure that finished products are available in the right quantities and at the right time so that materials and all individual parts and subassemblies can be completed according to the MPS.

2. In the net-change approach for updating net requirements, the MRP system recalculates requirements whenever necessary for all components.

3. The regeneration approach is less responsive to changes in requirements than the net-change approach.

4. Capacity requirements are computed by multiplying the number of units scheduled for production at a work center by the unit-resource requirements.

5. One of the principal attributes of MRP II is that it is user-transparent.

174 PART V: PLANNING AND SCHEDULING

6. JIT is well suited for job shops or other environments that require great production flexibility.

7. MRP is insensitive to capacity limitations.

8. Net-component requirements are calculated by subtracting the scheduled receipts and on-hand inventory from the gross-component requirements.

9. MRP is used to control inventories of independent demand items.

10. Assignment of priorities for components is **NOT** a function of MRP.

FILL IN THE BLANK

1. Inventories that support the production process are called _____ inventories.

2. A _____ of _____ shows the data for the makeup of each finished product.

3. The components at each level of a BOM hierarchy are _____ items for those at the next level.

4. Orders that have already been placed and are due to be delivered are called _____-_____.

5. The integration of capacity requirements, master scheduling, and MRP is often called a _____-_____ MRP system.

6. Capacity requirements information is usually found in a _____ report.

7. _____ _____ _____ is the process of planning all resources of a firm, including business planning, production planning, master production scheduling, material requirements planning, and capacity requirements planning.

8. _____ manufacturing is focused on moving material quickly through the productive resources of a manufacturing facility in response to market demand.

9. The process of "backing up" from the time the component or assembly is required by the amount of that item's lead time is called _____ _____.

10. The three key inputs to an MRP system are _____, _____, and _____.

❖ ❖ ❖ ❖ ❖ ❖ ❖ ❖ ❖ ❖

SELF-TEST PROBLEMS

1. One unit of finished product A is made of two units of B, three units of C, and two units of D. Each B is composed of one unit of E and two units of C. Each C is made of two units of F and one unit of D. And finally, each E is made of three units of D.

   A. Draw the bill of materials for product A.

   B. How many units of component D are required to produce 10 units of finished product A?

2. Complete the following MRP record for a low-level component using a lot size of 100 and a lead time of 2 periods. Assume on-hand inventory of 80 in period 1.

LS: 100 LT: 2	1	2	3	4	5	6
Gross Requirements		200	500	350		400
Scheduled Receipts	150		150		150	
On-hand Inventory						
Net Requirements						
Planned Order Releases						

3. The components used in the manufacture of finished product A are shown in the bill of materials below. The inventory record for the components is also provided. Now suppose, the master production schedule for product A requires production of 60, 30, 50 and 70 units of product A in periods 2, 3, 5, and 7 respectively.

   A. Determine the net requirements for component B and D.

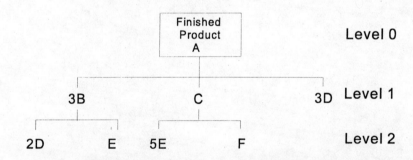

ITEM	ON-HAND	LEAD	LOT-SIZING	SCHEDULED	PERIOD
A	-	-	-	-	-
B	20	2	EOQ(80)	300	2
C	35	2	LFL	100	5
D	80	1	LFL	300	2,4
E	10	1	EOQ(50)	150	3
F	20	1	EOQ(100)	200	1,4

Key to Self-Test Questions

Multiple Choice

1. B
2. D
3. A
4. C
5. E
6. A
7. C
8. E
9. A
10. E

True/False

1. F
2. F
3. T
4. F
5. T
6. F
7. T
8. T
9. F
10. F

Fill in the Blank

1. manufacturing
2. bill of materials
3. parent
4. scheduled receipts
5. closed-loop
6. load
7. Manufacturing resource planning
8. Synchronous
9. time phasing
10. MPS, inventory records, BOM

KEY TO SELF-TEST PROBLEMS

1. A.

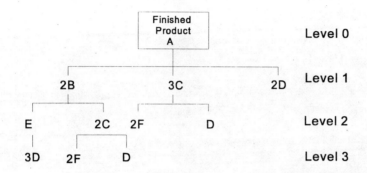

B. Number of D components required to produce 10 units of finished product A is:

(3 * 1 * 2 * 10) + (1 * 2 * 2 * 10) + (1 * 3 * 10) + (2 * 10) = 150

2.

LS: 100 LT: 2	1	2	3	4	5	6
Gross Requirements		200	500	350		400
Scheduled Receipts	150		150		150	
On-hand Inventory	80	230	30	80	30	180
Net Requirements			320	270		220
Planned Order Releases	400	300		300		

3. MRP record for component B:

From the bill of materials, 3 B's are required to make each finished product A. Therefore, the gross requirements are calculated as 3 times the requirements for finished product A (found in the MPS).

LS: 80 LT: 2	1	2	3	4	5	6	7
Gross Requirements		180	90		150		210
Scheduled Receipts		300					
On-hand Inventory	20	20	140	50	50	60	60
Net Requirements					100		150
Planned Order Releases			160		160		

MRP record for component D:

From the bill of materials, 3 D's are required to make each finished product A and 2 D's are required to make component B. Therefore, the gross requirements for component D is a combination of 3 times the requirements for finished product A (from the MPS) plus 2 times the planned order releases for component B (from the MRP record above).

LS: LFL LT: 1	1	2	3	4	5	6	7
Gross Requirements		180	410		470		210
Scheduled Receipts		300		300			
On-hand Inventory	80	80	200	0	300	0	0
Net Requirements			210		170		210
Planned Order Releases		210		170		210	

Chapter 18
Operations Scheduling and Production-Activity Control

LEARNING OBJECTIVES

Chapter 18 focuses on planning and scheduling. It begins by defining scheduling and production-activity control and addresses their relationship to the overall scope of production planning and scheduling. Finite capacity scheduling is discussed along with approaches for schedule development. The chapter also touches on special scheduling techniques. As you read, focus on the following questions:

- What is finite capacity scheduling (FCS)? How does it differ from MPS (master production scheduling) and MRP (material requirements planning)? How is a useful schedule developed?

- What is optimization-based scheduling? What is its objective? What are its advantages and disadvantages?

- What is the difference between scheduling and sequencing?

- What special cases of job-shop scheduling were discussed in the chapter? How can these special cases be applied?

- What are the difficulties of optimization-based approaches?

- What are dispatching rules and how are the rules for any given situation selected?

182   PART V: PLANNING AND SCHEDULING

✦ What is constraint-based scheduling? Can you explain what OPT is and how it works?

✦ What special scheduling problems might you encounter in manufacturing and service organizations and how might these problems be solved?

✦ Why is it so important to monitor progress while implementing schedules?

GLOSSARY

SCHEDULING	The assignment of priorities to manufacturing orders and allocation of work to specific work centers.
PRODUCTION-ACTIVITY CONTROL	Controls that provide data and information to production supervisors to enable them to ensure that materials and tools are available when needed, to track progress against planned requirements, and to make short-term adjustments when necessary.
FINITE CAPACITY SCHEDULING (FCS)	Scheduling based on given resource levels that cannot be changed in the short planning horizon that the scheduler faces.
MAKESPAN	A measure of the time needed to process a given set of jobs.
FLOWTIME	A measure of the amount of time a job spends in the shop.
DUE DATE	An internally determined shipping date.
TARDINESS	The measurement of the amount of time by which the completion time exceeds the due date.
LATENESS	The difference between the completion time and the due date. This number may be negative or positive.
SEQUENCING	The determining of the order in which jobs are processed.
SHORTEST PROCESSING TIME (SPT)	The minimization of average flowtime sequence by processing jobs in order of shortest processing time.
FLOWSHOP	A job shop in which all jobs have the same routing.
DISPATCHING RULES	Rules applied to the ranking of the order of jobs waiting to be processed at a machine in order to use capacity more effectively.

CHAPTER 18: OPERATIONS SCHEDULING AND PRODUCTION-ACTIVITY CONTROL

OPT — An approach to scheduling that entails obtaining a detailed description of the production system in a product network that reflects the reality of the manufacturing process.

DRUM-BUFFER-ROPE — The schedule development phase of constraint-based scheduling.

RUNOUT TIME — A calculation used in batch-production scheduling where inventory level is divided by demand rate. This tells the operations manager the length of time inventory will be available to meet demand.

SELF-TEST QUESTIONS

MULTIPLE CHOICE

1. Which of the following is **NOT** specified in scheduling?

    A. The timing of production.
    B. The sequence of production.
    C. The amount of work to be completed at any work center any time period.
    D. The priority of the work assignment.

2. The goal of the first-line supervisor is to:

    A. Meet customer-service objectives by completing orders on time.
    B. Minimize production costs by reducing work-in-process inventory.
    C. Minimize unnecessary machine setups.
    D. Maximize resource utilization by minimizing idle time and reducing in-plant congestion.
    E. All of the above are goals of first-line supervisors.

3. The categories of criteria for selecting a specific approach for FCS are:

    A. Makespan and flowtime.
    B. Shop-performance, due-date, and cost-based.
    C. Due dates, tardiness, and lateness.
    D. Makespan, flowtime, tardiness, and lateness.

184   PART V: PLANNING AND SCHEDULING

4. Due-date criteria contrasts with shop-performance by:

   A. Using measures that focus externally on customer satisfaction.
   B. Identifying relevant cost components and obtaining accurate estimates of their values.
   C. Trying to achieve high equipment utilization.
   D. Reducing WIP inventory.

5. Dispatching rules used in dynamic job-shop situations are usually based of:

   A. The attributes of the job.
   B. The characteristics of the shop itself at the particular time.
   C. Processing time.
   D. Number of operations involved.
   E. All of the above may be used in dispatching rules.

6. Which of the following is **NOT** a step in drum-buffer-rope scheduling?

   A. Identifying the constraint.
   B. Sequencing jobs on the constraint.
   C. Deciding on the size of the constraint buffers.
   D. Designing a product network.
   E. All of the above are part of drum-buffer-rope scheduling.

7. Which of the methods below is **NOT** a special scheduling problems for manufacturing and service organizations?

   A. Batch-production scheduling.
   B. Personnel scheduling.
   C. Computerized production control system scheduling.
   D. All of the above are special scheduling problems for manufacturing and service organizations.

8. Which of the following is **NOT** a means by which personnel scheduling attempts to match needs with available personnel?

   A. Determining the quantity of work to be done.
   B. Determining the staff required to perform the work.
   C. Evaluate the capabilities of the staff available.
   D. Match available personnel to staffing requirements.
   E. Create a work schedule.

CHAPTER 18: OPERATIONS SCHEDULING AND PRODUCTION-ACTIVITY CONTROL

9. Which of the following is a valid reason to alter an existing schedule?

   A. Material shortages.
   B. Work centers are backlogged.
   C. Labor turnovers.
   D. All of the above are valid reasons.
   E. Schedules should not be altered once set in motion.

10. Computerized production-control systems use the following inputs:

    A. Personnel file, inventory file, and equipment file.
    B. Route file, work-center file, and shop-order file.
    C. Equipment utilization file, order file, and inventory file.
    D. Product-flow file, work-center file, and capacity file.

TRUE/FALSE

1. Finite capacity scheduling (FCS) differs from MPS and MRP by basing schedules on resource constraints.

2. A short makespan aims to achieve high equipment utilization and resources by getting all jobs out of the shop quickly.

3. Shortest processing time (SPT) gives the smallest average flowtime of all scheduling rules but not the smallest average lateness.

4. Johnson's Rule refers to an algorithm used for finding a minimum makespan schedule.

5. One problem with optimization-based approaches is that they assume a dynamic situation for job availability.

6. Simulation is advantageous because it allows a manager to experiment with a model of the production system and choose what best applies for a particular set of criteria and shop conditions.

7. OPT works by sequentially considering how production resources should be used to meet requirements.

8. One of the rules governing the use of OPT software states that utilization and activation of a resource are synonymous.

9. The most difficult step in personnel scheduling is matching personnel to staffing requirements.

10. Short-term capacity fluctuations are avoidable and should not impact scheduling.

FILL IN THE BLANK

1. In _____ _____, the computer generates a schedule, identifies problems, and creates new schedules.

2. The category of criteria for selecting an approach for FCS that stresses start and end times of jobs is _____ _____.

3. One rule for scheduling on a single processor is the _____ rule, which dictates sequencing jobs in order of the earliest due date first.

4. If due dates must be met and tardiness cannot be tolerated, time phasing is often done _____.

5. Scheduling decisions must be made over _____.

6. The dispatching rule known as the _____ rule examines the sum of processing times for all operations not yet performed.

7. The _____ _____ is the ratio of the demand time of a job to the supply time.

8. The _____ is a system constraint or other critical resource that sets the pace or "beat" that drives the rest of the schedule in a constraint-based scheduling model.

9. When make-to-stock manufacturers produce different products on common facilities, these produced are usually produced in _____.

10. _____ is the process of assigning start and completion times to particular jobs.

CHAPTER 18: OPERATIONS SCHEDULING AND PRODUCTION-ACTIVITY CONTROL

SELF-TEST PROBLEMS

1. Six jobs are waiting to be processed on a single machine. Using the shortest processing time (SPT) rule, sequence these six jobs. Compute the flowtime, tardiness and lateness for each job. Compute the average flowtime, average tardiness, and average lateness for all jobs.

JOB	PROCESSING TIME	DUE DATE
1	13	40
2	9	11
3	17	51
4	10	18
5	15	42
6	12	35

2. A manufacturing procedure involves the processing on components in two operations on two different machines. The components must complete process one on machine one before going on to a second process on machine two. The present queue or waiting line is shown below.

JOB NUMBER	NUMBER OF COMPONENTS	SCHEDULED TIME ON MACHINE 1 (MIN./PIECE)	SCHEDULED TIME ON MACHINE 1 (MIN./PIECE)
176	135	2.0	1.5
183	100	1.5	2.5
195	160	1.5	1.0
207	75	2.5	1.0
213	125	1.5	2.0

Set up a schedule that will minimize makespan.

3. A paste manufacturer uses a single plant for filling, packaging, and shipping all four of its products. The inventory at the beginning of a particular week, the average demand, the production rate, and lot size are shown below (in 16 ounce cans). If runout time is used for scheduling this activity, how would the activity be scheduled during the first week?

Product	Inventory	Weekly Demand	Production Rate/Week	Lot Size
Pasta w/meat	50,000	40,000	100,000	72,000
Pasta w/o meat	40,000	35,000	125,000	35,000
Ravioli	35,000	25,000	75,000	20,000
Spaghetti	85,000	65,000	60,000	40,000

Chapter 18: Operations Scheduling and Production-Activity Control

Key to Self-Test Questions

Multiple Choice

1. D
2. E
3. B
4. A
5. E
6. E
7. C
8. C
9. D
10. B

True/False

1. T
2. T
3. F
4. T
5. F
6. T
7. T
8. F
9. T
10. F

Fill in the Blank

1. automated scheduling
2. shop-performance criteria
3. early-due-date
4. backwards
5. time
6. least-work-remaining
7. critical ratio
8. drum
9. batches
10. Scheduling

190 PART V: PLANNING AND SCHEDULING

KEY TO SELF-TEST PROBLEMS

1. Solution for *problem 1*.

JOB	FLOWTIME	DUE DATE	TARDINESS	LATENESS
2	9	11	0	-2
4	19	18	1	1
6	31	35	4	4
1	44	40	4	4
5	59	42	17	17
3	76	51	25	25
AVERAGE:	12.7		8.5	8.2

2. Solution for *problem 2*.

JOB	MACHINE 1	MACHINE 2
176	270	202.5
183	150	250
195	240	160
213	187.5	250
207	187.5	75

The sequence following Johnson's rule is 183-213-176-195-207.

3. Solution for *problem 3*.

PRODUCT	INVENTORY	DEMAND	RUNOUT TIME	
1	50,000	40,000	1.25	
2	40,000	35,000	1.14	← *schedule first*
3	35,000	25,000	1.40	
4	85,000	65,000	1.31	

CHAPTER 18: OPERATIONS SCHEDULING AND PRODUCTION-ACTIVITY CONTROL

Since the economic lot size for product 2 is 35,000 or only 28% of one week's run, the next decision arises after .28 weeks of production. The following table represents time = .28 weeks.

PRODUCT	INVENTORY	DEMAND	RUNOUT TIME
1	38,800	40,000	0.97	← *schedule next*
2	65,200	35,000	1.86
3	28,000	25,000	1.12
4	66,800	65,000	1.03

Schedule *Product 1* next. Since the economic lot size for product 1 is 72,000, which is 72% of one week's run, this will take us to the end of week 1. The following table represents the five products at the end of week 1.

PRODUCT	INVENTORY	DEMAND	RUNOUT TIME
1	82,000	40,000	2.05
2	40,000	35,000	1.14
3	10,000	25,000	0.40
4	20,000	65,000	0.31

Chapter 19
Project Planning, Scheduling, and Control

LEARNING OBJECTIVES

*C*hapter 19 introduces project management, the coordination of all activities surrounding a project. Project management requires the activities or events of a project be identified, planned, scheduled, and controlled. This chapter addresses attempts manage these events and introduces quantitative models that might help make this possible. Important questions to answer in this chapter are listed below.

- What is the scope of project planning and management?

- What factors are involved in project-management decisions?

- What are the four key skills a successful project manager must have?

- What are the two tools developed to assist project managers in scheduling?

- What are the steps of the project-planning process?

- What is involved in project definition? Resource planning? Project scheduling?

- What is a Gantt chart? How is it constructed and used?

- What is a critical path? Why is it important to a project?

- ✦ How can managers monitor performance of a project?

- ✦ How can planning and scheduling be accomplished with limited resources?

- ✦ How can resources change project completion times? How would you decide where to allocate these resources and how much to allocate?

Glossary

PROJECT	A set of tasks that must be performed in a specific order, on time, and within a budget.
PROJECT MANAGEMENT	All of the activities associated with planning, scheduling, and controlling projects.
ACTIVITY	Tasks that consume time.
EVENT	The points in time that represent the start or completion of a set of activities.
IMMEDIATE PREDECESSORS	One or more activities that must be completed before another activity is started.
PROJECT NETWORK	The graphical representation of a project's activities and events.
PERT/CPM NETWORK	This is used interchangeably with the term project network.
NODES	Circles on a graph that represent events.
BRANCH	Straight and curved arrows on a graph that connect nodes and represent activities.
ARC	Another name for branch.
DUMMY ACTIVITY	A fictitious activity with no activity time that is used to represent precedence or is used when two or more activities have the same starting and ending nodes.
OPTIMISTIC TIME	The amount of time that it will take to complete an activity if everything progresses in an ideal manner.
MOST PROBABLE TIME	The most likely time it will take to complete an activity under normal conditions.

PESSIMISTIC TIME	The amount of time that it will take to complete an activity if significant breakdowns and/or delays occur.
AVERAGE TIME	The computed time of an activity using the formula - $(a + 4m + b)/6$.
EXPECTED TIME	Another name for average time.
WORK PACKAGE	A set of activities under the control of one manager or department.
GANTT CHART	The graphical representation of a schedule that enables the manager to know what activities should be performed at a given time. It also allows the manager to monitor daily progress.
CRITICAL ACTIVITIES	The activities in a project that if delayed will force a delay in completion of the project.
CRITICAL PATH	The longest path through the project network. It contains the critical activities and determines the project completion time.
EARLIEST START TIME	The earliest time that an activity can be started.
LATEST FINISH TIME	The latest time that an activity can be finished without delaying the completion of the project.
SLACK	The amount of spare time an activity has. This is the difference between the soonest and the latest an activity can be started without delaying project completion.
CRASHING	The process of reducing activity times by increasing resources.

SELF-TEST QUESTIONS

MULTIPLE CHOICE

1. The three factors involved in all project-management decisions are:

    A. Identification, sequence and management of events.
    B. Time, resources, and cost.
    C. Project managers, early times, and late times.
    D. Planning, scheduling, and control.

2. The project-planning process consists of the following steps:

   A. Event identification, event sequencing, project scheduling, and project control.
   B. Planning, scheduling, monitoring, and controlling.
   C. Project definition, resource planning, project scheduling, and project control.
   D. All of the above are steps in the project-planning process.

3. The advantage of activity-on-node networks is:

   A. Dummy arcs are never necessary.
   B. Events have an explicit graphical representation.
   C. Arcs can be used to represent precedence relationships.
   D. It is not necessary to have complete a set of project activities in order to proceed with the planning process.

4. In order to estimate activity time accurately:

   A. Historical data can be is used to provide fairly accurate activity times.
   B. The nature of the activities may have low variability.
   C. The manager may have sufficient experience to estimate times.
   D. Any of the above can be true for accurate activity time estimation.

5. A schedule enables a manager to:

   A. Assign resources effectively.
   B. Monitor progress.
   C. Take corrective action.
   D. All of the above are true.

6. Which of the following statements is **NOT** true of the critical path?

   A. It is the longest path through the network.
   B. A delay for activities on the critical path will push back completion of the whole project.
   C. The critical path cannot contain dummy events.
   D. The critical path determines how long it will take to complete the entire project.

7. Which of the following is a method by which a manager could monitor performance of a project?

   A. Gantt chart.
   B. Budgetary control system.
   C. Determining cost overruns and underruns.
   D. All of the above are methods appropriate for monitoring performance of a project.

CHAPTER 19: PROJECT PLANNING, SCHEDULING, AND CONTROL

8. Which of the following statements is **NOT** true concerning crashing?

   A. Usually more resources are involved.
   B. Costs are generally higher.
   C. Project managers would be interested in reducing time on every activity.
   D. The benefits of decreased activity time must be weighed against increased project cost.

9. Which of the following statements is **NOT** true of project managers?

   A. They lead project activities.
   B. They are not found in technical areas.
   C. They plan and track progress of the work.
   D. They provide direction to project personnel.
   E. All of the above statements are true.

10. Which of the following is **NOT** true of skills needed by a successful project manager?

    A. A bias toward task completion.
    B. Administrative credibility with or without technical credibility.
    C. Interpersonal and political sensitivity.
    D. Leadership ability.
    E. All of the above are necessary skills.

TRUE/FALSE

1. The project manager's ability to supervise is more important than his or her ability to facilitate.

2. Today the distinction between PERT and CPM has largely disappeared.

3. Top-down budgeting is a hierarchical approach that begins with senior and mid-level managers.

4. Bottom-down budgeting is typically less accurate than top-down budgeting.

5. Gantt charts enable the operations manager to know exactly what activities should be performed at a given time.

6. The earliest start time for an activity leaving a particular node is equal to the smallest value of the earliest finish times for all activities entering the node.

198 PART V: PLANNING AND SCHEDULING

7. A noncritical activity, if delayed long enough, may become part of a new critical path.

8. A resource-loading chart shows the amount of resource required at any time by a particular schedule.

9. It is possible to determine optimal crashing by using a linear programming model of the problem.

10. Related activities under the control of one department or manager are often grouped together to form what are referred to as work packages.

FILL IN THE BLANK

1. _____ _____ are people who lead the project activities, plan and track progress of work, and provide direction to project personnel.

2. Networks in which nodes correspond to activities and arcs are used to represent precedence relationships are called _____ networks.

3. For scheduling purposes, the most important resource requirement is _____.

4. Two common budgeting practices are _____ and _____ budgeting.

5. The determination of when activities are to be performed is called _____.

6. A _____ in the network is a sequence of activities, performed in order, that starts at the beginning node and ends with the completion node.

7. _____ is the length of time an activity can be delayed without affecting the completion date for the project.

8. When resources are limited, a common objective is to _____ the project duration within resource constraints.

9. In the project-planning process, determining the activities that must be completed and the sequence required to perform them is called _____ _____.

10. Activity time if everything progresses in an ideal manner is called _____ time.

CHAPTER 19: PROJECT PLANNING, SCHEDULING, AND CONTROL

SELF-TEST PROBLEMS

1. The table below provides activities, their immediate predecessors, and their estimated completion times.

ACTIVITY	IMMEDIATE PREDECESSOR	ESTIMATED ACTIVITY TIME (WEEKS)
A	--	2
B	A	6
C	A	4
D	A	2
E	B	4
F	B,C,D	5
G	B	3
H	E,F	2

   A. Develop a PERT/CPM network for this model.

   B. Identify the critical path.

   C. Develop a detailed schedule for all activities in the project.

   D. What is the project-completion time?

2. Consider the project network below:

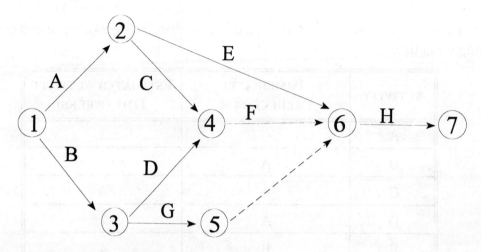

Managers have made estimates of the optimistic, most probable, and pessimistic times (in weeks) for the completion of the activities.

ACTIVITY	OPTIMISTIC TIME	MOST PROBABLE TIME	PESSIMISTIC TIME
A	3	5	7
B	6	8	10
C	7	10	12
D	8	9	10
E	5	7	11
F	3	4	6
G	2	5	9
H	1	3	5

A. Find the critical path.

B. Determine the expected project-completion time and the variance.

C. Find the probability that the project will be completed in 25 weeks.

Chapter 19: Project Planning, Scheduling, and Control

Key to Self-Test Questions

Multiple Choice

1. B
2. C
3. A
4. D
5. D
6. C
7. D
8. C
9. B
10. B

True/False

1. F
2. T
3. T
4. F
5. T
6. F
7. T
8. T
9. T
10. T

Fill in the Blank

1. Project managers
2. activity-on-node
3. time
4. top-down; bottom-up
5. scheduling
6. path
7. Slack
8. minimize
9. project definition
10. optimistic

KEY TO SELF-TEST PROBLEMS

1. A.

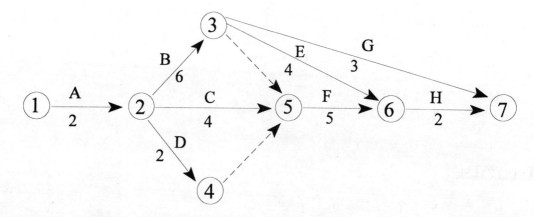

   B. A - B - F - H is the critical path.

   C.

Activity	Earliest Time	Earliest Finish	Latest Start	Latest Finish	Slack	Critical Path
A	0	2	0	2	0	✓
B	2	8	2	8	0	✓
C	2	6	4	8	2	
D	2	4	6	8	4	
E	8	12	9	13	1	
F	8	13	8	13	0	✓
G	8	11	12	15	4	
H	13	15	13	15	0	✓

   D. 15 weeks is the project-completion time.

2. A. B - D - F - H

   B. Projection-completion time is 24.2 weeks, with a variance of 1.11 weeks.

   C. The probability that the project will be completed within 25 weeks is 76.42%.

Supplement A
Computer Simulation

LEARNING OBJECTIVES

Computer Simulation is a technique used to describe real-world systems over time. This technique is an important tool in P/OM because it can be used to mimic a wide variety of situations that may not be approachable with most statistical or management science models. Quite often simulation is used in emulate a system that has a great deal of uncertainty. Once the simulation model is built, it becomes easy to perform "what if" analysis, where things change in the model and their impact can be determined without changing the actual system. As you read this supplement, answer the following questions:

- What is a system?

- What is the difference between a fixed-time and a next-event simulation model?

- Why are random numbers an important part of simulation? How are they used?

- How is a flowchart developed for a simulation model? How is that flowchart used?

- What is the problem with fixed-time simulation models?

GLOSSARY

FIXED-TIME SIMULATION MODEL A simulation model that increments time in fixed intervals.

PSEUDORANDOM NUMBERS Computer-generated numbers that have the properties of random numbers.

VALIDATION The process of determining that a model accurately represents the real-world system that it is designed to simulate.

NEXT-EVENT SIMULATION MODEL Models that increment time on the basis of the next event that will occur instead of using fixed-time intervals.

EVENT Any action that changes the simulation system.

SELF-TEST PROBLEMS

1. Elmo Manufacturing Company produces a product in a process of operations of 4 machines. These machines are not extremely reliable and frequently breakdown. The following data has been gathered by the production manager.

MACHINE BREAKDOWNS/WEEK	FREQUENCY
0	16
1	30
2	35
3	12
4	7

A. Develop a relative frequency distribution for the given data.

B. Use the random number on row 5 of *Appendix C* to simulate the machines for a 12-week period of time.

2. Nannette's Greenhouse specializes in raising carnations that are sold to local florists for $3.00 per dozen. The cost of growing and distributing the flowers is $2.00 per dozen. Any carnations left at the end of the day are sold to local restaurants and hotels for $.75 per dozen. The frequency distribution of the demand follows:

Dozens of Carnations:	25	30	35	40	45	50
Frequency:	10	14	18	11	8	4

Develop a probability distribution and using row 7 of *Appendix C* simulate 10 days of sales and determine the average daily profit if Nannette has 35 dozen ready to sale each day.

3. When a patient arrives at the doctor's office, the patient must check in with the receptionist, be evaluated by a nurse, see the doctor, and then pay the receptionist. The time it takes for each of these activities depends on how busy the office is and what health problem the patient is experiencing. The probability distribution for the time required to complete each of these activities is shown below:

ACTIVITY	ACTIVITY TIME (MINUTES)	PROBABILITY
Check-In	1	.35
	2	.30
	3	.25
	4	.10
See Nurse	3	.25
	4	.50
	5	.25
See Doctor	7	.45
	10	.35
	15	.20
Pay	2	.65
	5	.35

Simulate 5 patients coming and going from the doctor's office (using row 6 of *Appendix C*) and calculate average time at the office.

4. *Refer to Problem 1.* The cost of repairing a machine (labor plus lost productivity) is $100 per hour. Using the probability distribution below for repair times and row 13 of *Appendix C*, simulate 5 weeks of operation and calculate total repair costs.

REPAIR TIME (HOURS)	PROBABILITY
1	.25
2	.40
3	.35

5. The Chandler Aircraft operates a large number of computerized plotting machines. The computerized plotters consist of a microcomputer connected to 4-by-5-foot flat table with a series of ink pens suspended above it. When a sheet of clear plastic or paper is properly placed on the table, the computer directs a series of horizontal and vertical pen movements until the desired figure is drawn. The plotting machines are highly reliable, with the exception of the four sophisticated ink pens that are built in. The pens constantly clog. When this occurs, the plotter is unusable.

Currently, Chandler replaces each pen as it fails. The service manager has proposed replacing all four pens every time one fails. This should cut down the frequency of plotter failures. At present, it takes one hour to replace one pen. All four pens could be replaced in two hours. The total cost of a plotter being unusable is $100 per hour. Each pen costs $15.

If only one pen is replaced each time a clog or jam occurs, the following breakdown data are thought to be valid:

HOURS BETWEEN PLOTTER FAILURES IF ONE PEN REPLACED DURING A REPAIR	PROBABILITY
25	.10
35	.20
45	.25
55	.30
65	.15

Based on the service manager's estimates, if all four pens are replaced each time one pen fails, the probability distribution between failure is:

HOURS BETWEEN PLOTTER FAILURES IF FOUR PENS REPLACED DURING A REPAIR	PROBABILITY
125	.20
135	.35
145	.25
155	.15
165	.05

Simulate for 400 hours using row 1 of *Appendix C* to determine the best policy. Should the firm replace one pen or all four pens on a plotter each time a failure occurs?

KEY TO SELF-TEST PROBLEMS

1. A.

BREAKDOWNS	RELATIVE FREQUENCY	RANDOM NUMBERS
0	.16	00-15
1	.30	16-45
2	.35	46-80
3	.12	81-92
4	.07	93-99

B.

WEEK	RANDOM NUMBER	BREAKDOWNS
1	55	2
2	36	1
3	30	1
4	74	2
5	49	2
6	34	1
7	83	3
8	51	2
9	52	2
10	90	3
11	76	2
12	61	2

2.

Relative Dozens Sold	Relative Frequency	Numbers
25	.15	00-14
30	.22	15-36
35	.28	37-64
40	.17	65-81
45	.12	82-93
50	.06	94-99

Day	Random Number	Number Demand	Sold ($3)	Sold ($.75)	Profit
1	13	25	25	10	12.50
2	18	30	30	5	23.75
3	62	35	35	0	35.00
4	94	50	35	0	35.00
5	31	30	30	5	23.75
6	88	45	35	0	35.00
7	19	30	30	5	23.75
8	00	25	25	10	12.50
9	45	35	35	0	35.00
10	88	45	35	0	35.00
				Average Profit Per Day →	$27.12

3.

Activity	Activity Time (Minutes)	Random Numbers
Check In	1	00-34
	2	35-64
	3	65-89
	4	90-99
See Nurse	3	00-24
	4	25-74
	5	75-99
See Doctor	7	00-44
	10	45-79
	15	80-99
Pay	2	00-64
	5	65-99

Random Number	Check In	Random Number	Nurse	Random Number	Doctor	Random Number	Pay	Total Time
69	3	39	4	39	7	27	2	16
85	3	49	4	90	15	25	2	24
84	3	47	4	42	7	04	2	16
83	3	03	3	78	10	87	5	21
61	2	82	5	69	10	33	2	19
Average Time Per Patient →								19.2 minutes

4.

Repair Time (Hours)	Random Numbers
1	00-24
2	25-64
3	65-99

Random Number	Number of Machines that Break Down	Random Number	Repair Time
70	2	50	2
	25	2	
32	1	25	2
03	0		
65	2	50	2
	59	2	
15	0		
Total Repair Cost After 5 Weeks = $1,000			

5. For present policy:

Repair Between Failures	Random Numbers
25	00-09
35	10-29
45	30-54
55	55-84
65	85-99

Random Number	Time Between	Total Time	Cost
63	55	55	$115
27	35	90	115
15	35	125	115
99	65	190	115
86	65	255	115
71	55	310	115
74	55	365	115
45	45	410	115
Average Cost Per Hour of Operation = $920/410 = $2.24			

For Proposed policy:

Repair Between Failures	Random Numbers
125	00-19
135	20-54
145	55-79
155	80-94
165	95-99

Random Number	Time Between	Total Time	Cost
11	125	125	$260
02	125	250	260
15	125	375	260
14	125	500	260
Average Cost Per Hour of Operation = $1040/500 = $2.08			

The policy proposed by the service manager is cheaper.

Supplement B
Decision Analysis

LEARNING OBJECTIVES

Decision analysis explores possible decision alternatives and their payoffs under uncertain future conditions and attempts to select the best course of action. This supplement introduces basic concepts and procedures of decision analysis. As you read the supplement, you should be able to answer the following questions:

- ✦ What are states of nature?

- ✦ How are payoffs determined? How are these used to create a payoff table?

- ✦ How might a decision be made without probabilities?

- ✦ What is an expected value? How is it calculated?

- ✦ What is a decision tree?

- ✦ What is the expected value of perfect information and how is it calculated? For what might this value be used?

Glossary

Payoff Table A table that shows the payoff, or profit, for each decision alternative under each possible state of nature.

Maximax An optimistic approach to decision making without probabilities where the decision selected is the course of action that has the highest possible payoff among all states of nature.

Maximin A conservative approach to decision making without probabilities where the decision selected maximizes the minimum payoff.

Minimax Regret A decision criteria for decision making without probabilities that minimizes the maximum opportunity loss associated with the states of nature.

Regret The cost of a lost opportunity.

Opportunity-Loss Matrix A matrix that shows the difference between the best possible payoff and any other payoff for each state of nature.

Decision Tree The graphical representation of the sequence of decisions and the states of nature.

Nodes Intersections or junction points in a decision tree.

Branches Arcs or connectors between nodes, representing a decision or a state of nature.

SELF-TEST PROBLEMS

1. Suppose a decision maker faced with three decision alternatives and three states of nature develops the payoff table shown below.

DECISION	STATES OF NATURE		
	S1	S2	S3
D1	$-5,000	$15,000	$20,000
D2	2,000	8,000	6,000
D3	6,000	6,000	5,000

   Use maximax, maximin, and minimax-regret criteria to evaluate the payoff table.

2. PatChem Chemical Corporation is considering expanding their present manufacturing facility. This would require a large capital expenditure. The expansion is necessary if future demand experiences the amount of growth PatChem anticipates. Below is a payoff table projecting future earnings.

DECISION	STATES OF NATURE		
	INCREASED DEMAND	STABLE DEMAND	DECREASED DEMAND
Expand	$120,000	$70,000	$-30,000
No Expansion	60,000	40,000	20,000

A. Construct a decision tree for this problem.

B. Determine the best decisions using maximax, maximin, and minimum-regret.

C. Assume the probability of demand increasing is 0.3, of demand remaining the same is 0.5, and of demand decreasing is 0.2. What would the best decision be using EMV criteria?

3. A local real estate investor in Long Boat Key has purchased land and is considering building a condominium complex, a restaurant, or a hotel. Profits from these ventures will depend on future interest rates. These interest rates affect building loans, as well as loans home owners would need to purchase condominiums. The following payoff table shows the profit or loss that could result for each investment.

DECISION	STATES OF NATURE		
	INCREASED RATES	STABLE RATES	DECREASED
Condos	$1,500,000	$1,950,000	$2,200,000
Restaurant	750,000	875,000	990,000
Hotel	1,600,000	1,750,000	1,800,000

If P(Increased) = .4, P(Stable) = .5, and P(Decreased) = .1, what decision is recommended by the EMV criterion?

4. Randall Brothers Dairy produces, among other dairy products, cheddar cheese. The cheese is sold for $3.00 per pound; the cost of producing the cheese is $2.00 per pound. Any cheese left at the end of the day is sold to a local deli for $.75 per pound. The estimated cost of customer ill will is demand is not met is $1.00 per pound. The expected daily demand for cheese is shown below.

Daily Demand	Probability
200	.05
220	.10
240	.25
260	.30
280	.20
300	.10

A. Develop a payoff table for this problem.

B. How many pounds of cheese should the dairy produce daily?

5. The real estate investor *(Problem 3)* is considering hiring a consultant to study the economy make a recommendation as to which option would be most profitable. The consultant wants $25,00 for his report. What should the investor do?

KEY TO SELF-TEST PROBLEMS

1. maximax selects D1
   maximin selects D3
   minimax-regret selects D1

2. A.

   ```
                        S₁
                  ┌──────── 120,000
              D₁  │    S₂
         ┌───────②──────── 70,000
         │        │    S₃
         │        └──────── -30,000
      [1]│
         │             S₁
         │        ┌──────── 60,000
         │    D₂  │    S₂
         └───────③──────── 40,000
                  │    S₃
                  └──────── 20,000
   ```

   B. maximax selects Expand
      maximin selects No Expansion
      minimum-regret selects Expand

   C. EMV (Expand) = $65,000
      EMV (No Expansion) = $42,000
      EMV selects Expand

3. EMV (Condo) = $1,795,000
   EMV (Restaurant) = $ 836,500
   EMV (Hotel) = $1,695,000
   EMV selects Condominiums

4. A.

PRODUCTION	DEMAND					
	.05 200	.10 220	.25 240	.30 260	.20 280	.10 300
200	200	180	160	140	120	100
220	175	220	200	180	160	140
240	150	195	240	220	200	180
260	125	170	215	260	240	220
280	100	145	190	235	280	260
300	75	120	165	210	255	300

B. EMV(200) = $144.00
    EMV(220) = $180.80
    EMV(240) = $211.00
    EMV(260) = $225.00
    EMV(280) = $219.50
    EMV(300) = $201.00

   EMV selects production of 260 pounds of cheese daily.

5. The expected monetary value of this decision with perfect information is $1,835,000. Without perfect information, the monetary value is $1,795,000. The value of the expected payoff is increased by $40,000. The real estate investor would be willing to pay $25,000 for the advise of a good consultant.

Supplement C
Waiting-Line Models

LEARNING OBJECTIVES

Waiting lines are a concern to all managers. However, to eliminate waiting means that service capacity must be increased. Sometimes this can only be done at a considerable cost. This supplement discusses queuing, or waiting-line, theory. There are different types of models that can handle queuing analysis. After reading this supplement, you should be able to discuss the following:

- When are analytical models used versus simulation?

- What are operating characteristics? Can you list these characteristics?

- What distribution describes arrival rates? What are the characteristics of that distribution?

- What distribution describes service time?

- What is queue discipline?

- What are the differences between single-channel and multiple-channel waiting-line models?

- Can you discuss the need for economic analysis of waiting-line models?

Glossary

Queue
A waiting line.

Poisson Probability Distribution
A discrete probability distribution used to describe the arrival pattern. This distribution is used when the number of trials is very small and the probability of success on any one trial is very small.

Mean Arrival Rate
The average number of arrivals into the systems for some specific time frame.

Exponential Mean Service Rate
The average number that can be serviced by the system in some specific time frame.

Single-Channel Waiting Line
A system in which each server has his/her own waiting line. There may be many servers, but there is a separate waiting line for each of them.

Utilization Factor
The probability that a server is busy, or the percent of the time that a server is busy. This is calculated by dividing arrival rate by service rate.

Multiple-Channel Waiting Line
A system in which there is more than one server helping with each waiting line. Arrivals will wait in one line, and move to the first server free for service.

Self-Test Questions

Multiple Choice

1. Which of the following would **NOT** be considered an operating characteristics?

    A. Percentage of the time or probability that the service facilities are idle.
    B. Probability of a specific number of units in the system.
    C. Average arrival rate.
    D. Average time in the waiting line.
    E. Average number of units in the system.

2. In a single-channel waiting-line model:

   A. The waiting line feeds into more than one service facility.
   B. Arrival pattern follows the Poisson probability distribution.
   C. Service times follow the Poisson probability distribution.
   D. Queue discipline is random.

3. To analyze a single-channel waiting-line model with poisson arrivals and exponential service times:

   A. Arrival rate must equal service rate.
   B. Arrival rate must be greater than service rate.
   C. When dividing arrival rate by service rate, the answer must be less than 1.
   D. When dividing arrival rate by service rate, the answer must be greater than 1.

4. Which of the following statements is **NOT** true concerning the assumptions of a multiple-channel waiting-line model?

   A. The waiting line has at least two unique channels.
   B. Arrivals follow a Poisson distribution.
   C. Service times follow an exponential distribution.
   D. Arrivals wait in a single line and then move to the first open channel for service.

TRUE/FALSE

1. Simulation models are better equipped to capture the dynamic behavior of a waiting-line system over time.

2. The system includes the waiting line plus the service facility.

3. Queue discipline refers to behavior in the queue itself.

4. In the economic analysis of waiting lines we seek to use information provided by the waiting-line model to develop a cost model for the waiting line under study.

FILL IN THE BLANK

1. In a queuing system, performance measures are also called _____ _____.

2. When each arrival is independent of other arrivals and we cannot predict when they will occur, arrival rate is said to follow a _____ pattern.

3. The length of time needed to process an arrival is called _____ time.

4. The _____ cost of waiting is an estimate of the reasonable value of losing future revenue should a customer refrain from using a service again because of long waiting times.

Self-Test Problems

1. Customers arrivals in a single server channel queue at the cash register in a grocery store at an average rate of 28 per hour. Service rate is 30 per hour.

    A. What is the probability that the cashier is idle?

    B. How long will a customer wait for service on the average?

    C. How long is the average line?

    D. On the average how many customers are at the cash register?

2. Students arrive at the advising center and form a single-channel waiting line. On the average, the advisor can talk to 5 students in an hour. Usually four students come into the center per hour.

    A. What is the probability that the advisor has no students at the center?

    B. How long is a student at the center?

    C. On the average, how many students are in the advising center?

    D. How long is the average wait to see the advisor?

3. The Newcomb Corporation must make a decision regarding its policy for hiring repairmen to fix machines that break down at an average rate of 4 per hour. Nonproductive time on any of the machines is costing the firm $10 per hour. The firm can hire repairmen of 2 different types: one is slow but inexpensive (8.50 per hour), the other is fast but expensive (15.00 per hour). The slow repairman will repair machines at an average rate of 6 per hour, whereas the fast repairman will repair machines at a rate of 8 per hour.

   A. Compute the waiting line statistics for each repairman.

   B. Which repairman provides the lowest operating cost?

4. The Riverview Clinic has one general practitioner who sees patients daily. An average of 5 patients arrive at the clinic per hour. The doctor usually spends 10 minutes with each patient. Because patients are generally ill when they come to the clinic, the doctor would like waiting time to be no longer than 30 minutes. Is this goal being met?

5. Spee Dee Dry Cleaner has a drive-in service window. It generally takes 2 minutes for the clerk to fill out a dry cleaning slip and take the clothes from the customer. Approximately 25 customer come to the store in one hour. To improve service, Spee Dee is considering opening another window on the other side of the store. The second window will have the same service rate. The cars will be divided between the two windows. Compare the two systems.

6. The Tristate Manufacturing Company is considering a two-channel system in which one assembly line would feed two drill presses. Each press can process 60 units per hour. The partially completed products arrive at the workstation at a rate of 100 per hour.

   A. What is the probability that the workstation will be idle?

   B. How many products are waiting to be processed on the average?

   C. How long is waiting time the average?

   D. How many products are at the workstation?

KEY TO SELF-TEST QUESTIONS

MULTIPLE CHOICE

1. C
2. B
3. C
4. A

TRUE/FALSE

1. T
2. T
3. F
4. T

FILL IN THE BLANK

1. operating characteristics
2. random
3. service
4. imputed

KEY TO SELF-TEST PROBLEMS

1. A. $P_o = .17$
   B. $W_q = .47$ hour or 28.2 minutes
   C. $L_q = 13.1$ students
   D. $L = 14$ students

2. A. $P_o = .20$
   B. $W = 1$ hour
   C. $L = 4$ students
   D. $W_q = .80$ hour or 48 minutes

3. For the slower repairman:
   A. Po = .33
      L = 2 machines
      Lq = 1.33 machines
      W = .50 hour or 30 minutes
      Wq = .33 hour or 20 minutes

   For the faster repairman:
   A. Po = .50
      L = 1 machine
      Lq = .5 machine
      W = .25 hours or 15 minutes
      Wq = .125 hours or 7.5 minutes

   B. Operating cost for slower repairman:
      (.50 * $10 * 4) + $8.50 = $28.50 *per hour*
      (*W * penalty cost * no. breakdowns per hour*) + *salary*

   Operating cost for faster repairman:
      (.25 * $10 * 4) + $15 = $25.00 *per hour*

   Hire the faster repairman.

4. Wq = .83 hour or 49.8 minutes
   The goal of holding waiting time to 30 minutes or less is not being realized.

5. The system with one window:
   Po = .17
   L = 5 customers
   Lq = 5.2 customers
   W = .20 hours or 12 minutes
   Wq = .17 hours or 10 minutes

The system with two windows:
Po = .58
L = .71 customers
Lq = .30 customers
W = .057 hours or 3.4 minutes
Wq = .023 hours or 1.4 minutes

The system with two windows moves much faster for the customers. However, there is also a lot of idle time for the workers manning the windows. More analysis should be done comparing the cost of the two systems.

6. Po = .09
Lq = 3.77 products
Wq = .038 hours or 2.26 minutes
L = 5.44 products

Supplement D
Linear Programming

LEARNING OBJECTIVES

Linear programming is one of the most widely used models in management science. This is especially true in the area of operations management. Solutions to these problems allow an optimal allocation of resources while meeting an objective of maximizing or minimizing some quantity, usually profit or cost respectively. This supplement discusses developing and solving linear programming problems. You should finish this supplement with a basic understanding of the following:

- ✦ What are decision variables? An objective function? Constraints?

- ✦ What is the difference between a feasible solution and an optimal solution?

- ✦ How is an optimal solution found?

- ✦ How is a linear programming model formulated?

- ✦ How is this formulation used to create a graphical representation of the problem?

- ✦ What are the steps for finding the optimal solution for a graph? What are extreme points?

- ✦ How can Microsoft Excel be used to find optimal solutions for linear programming?

✦ What is the simplex solution method? What are the main steps of this method?

GLOSSARY

OBJECTIVE FUNCTION	The linear equation that states the objective of the linear programming problem. For most linear programming problems, the goal is to minimize cost or maximize profit, with the profit or cost being measured by the objective function.
SOLUTION	The set of values assigned to variables in a problem.
FEASIBLE SOLUTION	A solution that satisfies all the constraints placed on the linear programming problem.
OPTIMAL SOLUTION	A feasible solution that meets the objective of maximizing profit or minimizing cost.
NONNEGATIVITY CONSTRAINTS	A set of constraints placed on every linear programming problem that requires all variables to have a value greater than or equal to zero.
LINEAR PROGRAM	A math model that contains an objective function and constraints, all expressed in linear equations using decision variables.
CONSTRAINT FUNCTIONS	The left hand side of the constraint expressing resource usage in terms of decision variables.
LINEAR FUNCTION	A function in which each variable appears in a separate term and is raised to the first power.
SIMPLEX METHOD	An algorithm that systematically searches among corner points until it identifies an optimal solution or determine that none exist.
SLACK VARIABLE	A variable used in less-than-or-equal-to constraints to convert them to equality equations.
SIMPLEX TABLEAU	The representation of a linear programming problem in tabular form. This table will then be used for solation with the simplex method.

SELF-TEST PROBLEMS

1. Solve the following linear programming model graphically.

$$\max 5X1 + 10X2$$

$$2X1 + 4X2 \leq 40$$
$$X1 + X2 \leq 15$$
$$X1 \geq 8$$
$$X1, X2 \geq 0$$

A. Find the optimal solution.

B. How many extreme points are there? What are the values of X1 and X2 at each extreme point?

C. Which of these extreme points is the optimal solution point?

D. What is profit at this point?

E. If the objective function changed to 30X1 + 10X2, what would the optimal solution be?

2. Olde Style Furniture Company manufacturers tables and chairs. Profit per table is $250, while profit per chair is $135. Tables require 50 pounds of wood, chairs require 15. It takes 8 hours to make a table and 10 to make a chair. Olde Style only has 450 pounds of wood available each day, and enough laborers to supply 80 hours of work daily. Demand for chairs is limited to 6 chairs a day.

   A. What is the linear programming model?

   B. How many tables and chairs are made at the optimal solution? How much profit is generated at this solution?

   C. How much is used of each resource? How much is not used?

3. The Valley Wine Company produces 2 kinds of wine: Valley Nectar and Valley Red. The wines are produced in gross (144 bottles) from grapes, and the company has 64 tons of grapes this season to use in wine production. It takes 4 tons of grapes to produce a gross of Valley Nectar and 8 tons of grapes to produce a gross of Valley Red. However, production is limited by the availability of storage space for aging and processing time. Storing 144 bottles (a gross) of either wine requires 5 square yards of storage space, and only 50 square yards are available. Valley Nectar requires 15 hours of processing time per gross, Valley Red takes 8 hours. Only 120 hours of processing time are available. Profit is $9000 per gross of Valley Nectar, $12,000 for Valley Red.

   A. What is the linear programming model?

   B. What are the optimum production quantities?

   C. What constraint lines crossed to form the optimal extreme point?

   D. Are all the resources used completely? If not, which ones have left over quantities?

   E. What is the most profit that Valley Wine Company can hope to make?

4. Sleep-E-Z Clock, Inc. produces alarm clocks. They have three clocks that make up the majority of their sales. One clock has large digital read out, for people who have trouble seeing a standard size clock face at night. Another is a stripped down model that has time and alarm only. The last clock has a radio and standard size digital read out. These products have the following resource requirements.

PRODUCT	RESOURCE REQUIREMENTS	
	COST/UNIT	LABOR HOURS/UNIT
Clock 1	$10	3
Clock 2	5	2
Clock 3	9	3

Sleep-E-Z has a daily production budget of $2000, and a maximum of 660 hours of labor. Maximum customer demand is 200 for *clock 1*, 300 for *clock 2*, and 400 for *clock 3*. *Clock 1* sells for $18, *clock 2* for $9, and *clock 3* for $13.

A. What is the linear programming model?

B. Find the optimal solution. How many of each type of clock are manufactured? What is profit at the optimal solution?

C. How much is used of each resource and how much slack do you have for each resource?

242 SUPPLEMENTARY CHAPTERS

KEY TO SELF-TEST PROBLEMS

1. A.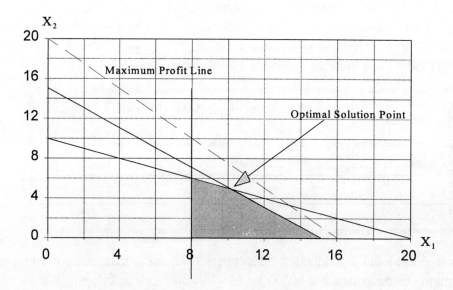

   B. There are three extreme points. Their values are 8,5; 10,5; and 15,0.

   C. Point 10,5.

   D. Profit is $100.

   E.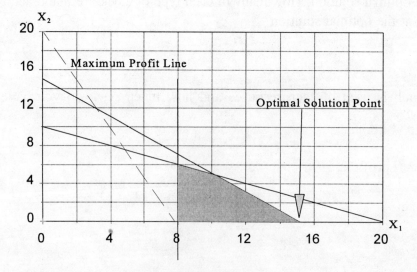

   The optimal solution point would be point 15,0.

2. A.
$$\max 250X1 + 135X2$$
$$50X1 + 15X2 \le 450$$
$$8X1 + 10X2 \le 80$$
$$X2 \le 6$$
$$X1, X2 \ge 0$$

B. At the optimal solution point, Olde Style will produce 8.7 tables and 1.05 chairs for a total profit of $2313.16.

C.

Resource	Used	Remaining
Wood	450 lbs	0 lbs
Labor	80 hours	0 hours
Demand	1.05 customers	4.95 customers

3. A.
$$\max 9000X1 + 12000X2$$
$$4X1 + 8X2 \le 64$$
$$5X1 + 5X2 \le 50$$
$$15X1 + 8X2 \le 120$$
$$X1, X2 \ge 0$$

B. Produce 4 gross of Valley Nectar and 6 gross of Valley Red.

C. The constraints dealing with limitations on grapes and storage capacity.

D. There are 12 hours of production time that are not used.

E. Maximum profit is $108,000.

4. A.
$$\max 8X1 + 4X2 + 4X3$$
$$10X1 + 5X2 + 9X3 \le 2000$$
$$3X1 + 2X2 + 3X3 \le 660$$
$$X1 \le 200$$
$$X2 \le 300$$
$$X3 \le 400$$
$$X1, X2, X3 \ge 0$$

B. Produce 200 of *clock 1*, but none of either *clock 2 or 3*.
Profit at this optimal solution is $1600.

C.

Resource	Used	Remaining
Budget	$2,000	$0
Labor	600 hours	60 hours
Demand:		
Clock 1	200	0 customers
Clock 2	0	200 customers
Clock 3	0	400 customers

Supplement E
Transportation Problem

LEARNING OBJECTIVES

This supplement discusses a special type of linear programming problem in which goods or services are shipped around a geographic area from specific points of origin to several demand locations. In moving these goods and services, the objective is to satisfy demand while not straying from the limitations of supply, usually at a minimum shipping cost. This model is called the ***transportation problem***. While reading this supplement, concentrate on the following questions:

- What is a transportation tableau? What information can you glean from a tableau?

- How do you know when a transportation solution is optimal?

- How do you deal with inequities in supply and demand?

- How are unacceptable shipping routes handled?

Glossary

Transportation Problem — A special type of linear programming problem in which goods and services are shipped from several supply points to several demand destinations.

Transportation Tableau — A table that shows points of origins, destinations, supply, and demand for a transportation problem. It is used to perform necessary calculations to solve the transportation model.

Cell — A block within the transportation tableau that shows shipping from a specific origin to a specific destination as well as the cost involved.

Dummy Destination — An artificial demand destination that is added to the transportation tableau in an attempt to balance supply and demand within a transportation problem when total supply exceeds total demand.

Dummy Origin — An artificial supply destination that is added to the transportation tableau in an attempt to balance supply and demand within a transportation problem when total demand exceeds total supply.

SELF-TEST PROBLEMS

1. Three steel mills in different cities supply manufacturing plants in two cities. Supply, demand, and shipping costs (in dollars per ton) are shown below.

MILLS	MANUFACTURING LOCATIONS		
	CITY 1	CITY 2	SUPPLY
1	14	16	150
2	11	18	210
3	17	20	160
DEMAND:	350	170	

Set up the transportation tableau and find an optimal solution.

2. A manufacturing firm produces diesel engines in three locations and ships them to buyers in three different cities. Using the information below, find the optimal solution.

FACTORIES	BUYERS FOR DIESEL ENGINES			SUPPLY
	CITY 1	CITY 2	CITY 3	
1	75	85	70	50
2	93	110	89	75
3	98	115	120	80
DEMAND	100	90	75	

3. Cotton is stored in three warehouses awaiting shipment to four mills. A truckers' strike prevents shipment from *Warehouse 2* to *Mill 2*. Shipping costs are given per truckload.

WAREHOUSES	MILLS REQUESTING COTTON				SUPPLY
	MILL 1	MILL 2	MILL 3	MILL 4	
1	100	125	115	130	200
2	95	105	120	118	350
3	117	128	130	125	175
DEMAND	250	125	200	100	

A. Find the optimal solution.

B. Which warehouse is left with excess inventory? Why was that warehouse selected to be the location with cotton left over in inventory?

4. Peaches are picked and stored in four warehouses before the fruit is shipped to stores in three cities.

WAREHOUSES	CITIES REQUESTING PEACHES			SUPPLY
	CITY 1	CITY 2	CITY 3	
1	150	167	175	125
2	168	200	225	225
3	185	235	215	205
DEMAND	175	250	210	

A. Using the costs per truckload shown above, find the optimal solution.

B. How would your solution change if *City 1* does not want peaches from *Warehouse 2*?

C. Would your solution change if *City 3* increased their order to 225 truckloads of peaches?

Key to Self-Test Problems

1. Transportation - Optimal Solution - Tableau Output

	City 1	City 2	U(I)\Supply
Mill 1	14	16 150	150
Mill 2	11 210	18	210
Mill 3	17 140	20 20	160
V(J) Demand	350	170	

Total Cost = $7,490

2. Transportation - Optimal Solution - Tableau Output

	City 1	City 2	City 3	U(I)\Supply
Factory 1	75	85 30	70 20	50
Factory 2	93 20	110	89 55	75
Factory 3	98 80	115	120	80
Dummy	0	0 60	0	60
V(J) Demand	100	90	75	

Total Cost = $18,545.0000

3. A. Transportation - Optimal Solution - Tableau Output

	Mill 1	Mill 2	Mill 3	Mill 4	Dummy	U(I)\Supply
Warehouse 1	100	125	115 / 200	130	0	200
Warehouse 2	95 / 250	120	120	118 / 100	0	3 / 350
Warehouse 3	117	128 / 125	130	125	0 / 50	3.000 / 175
V(J) Demand	250	125	200	100	50	

Total Cost = $74,550.0000

B. *Warehouse 3* has 50 truckloads of cotton left over after shipping. Since supply exceeded demand by 50 truckloads, excess cotton inventory had to be left in one of the warehouses. *Warehouse 3* was chosen because the objective is to minimize cost and it had the highest shipping costs of all the warehouses.

4. A. Transportation - Optimal Solution - Tableau Output

	City 1	City 2	City 3	U(I)\Supply
Warehouse 1	150	167 / 125	175	125
Warehouse 2	167 / 175	200 / 50	225	225
Warehouse 3	185	235	215 / 205	205
Dummy	0	0 / 75	0 / 5	80
V(J) Demand	175	250	210	

Total Cost = $104,175.0000

B. Transportation - Optimal Solution - Tableau Output

	City 1	City 2	City 3	U(I)\Supply
Factory 1	150	167 / 25	175 / 100	125
Factory 2	200	200 / 225	225	225
Factory 3	185 / 175	235	215 / 30	205
Dummy	0	0	0 / 80	80
V(J) Demand	175	250	210	

Total Cost = $105,500.0000

C. Demand exceeds supply in this problem by 80 truckloads. *City 3* requests 210 truckloads and only receives 130 because of shortages and because of City 3's shipping costs. Increasing their order by any amount will not change the solution, it will only increase the quantity of peaches that they will not receive.